Hermon Carey Bumpus

HERMON CAREY BUMPUS

Yankee Naturalist

by
HERMON CAREY BUMPUS, JR.

THE UNIVERSITY OF MINNESOTA PRESS
Minneapolis

Copyright 1947 by the
UNIVERSITY OF MINNESOTA

All rights reserved. No part of this book
may be reproduced in any form without
the written permission of the publisher.
Permission is hereby granted to reviewers
to quote brief passages in a review to be
printed in a magazine or newspaper.

PRINTED BY THE GEORGE BANTA PUBLISHING COMPANY
MENASHA, WISCONSIN

Preface

THE life story of Hermon Carey Bumpus was so out of the ordinary and intimately touched and influenced so many persons that his good friend Dr. A. D. Mead volunteered to record it. Unfortunately, circumstances made it necessary for Dr. Mead to give up the work after he had accumulated much of the material for this biography.

Dr. Herbert E. Walter, a friend and former associate of both Dr. Bumpus and Dr. Mead, then generously offered to take over. With skill and patience he articulated the parts of this biography, but he too was prevented from completing the project. Of his work he wrote: "It has been a pleasant task, with abundant original documentary sources at hand, to attempt a compilation of the fascinating adventures of this man whom so many friends remember with affection and respect. To do this has been a willing labor of love."

With deep appreciation of the work done by Dr. Mead and Dr. Walter, I have endeavored to build on the foundation laid by them, adding material and memories that came to me through a close association with my father for over fifty years.

HERMON CAREY BUMPUS, JR.

Table of Contents

I. ANCESTRY AND BOYHOOD....................	3
II. AS STUDENT AND BEGINNING TEACHER.....	17
III. WOODS HOLE.................................	25
IV. BROWN UNIVERSITY, 1890–1900...............	35
V. THE AMERICAN MUSEUM OF NATURAL HISTORY, 1900–1910....................................	54
VI. FRIEND TO THE GAEKWAR OF BARODA.....	73
VII. UNIVERSITY ADMINISTRATOR, Wisconsin 1911–1914, Tufts 1915–1919................................	79
VIII. BUILDER AND GARDENER..................	92
IX. TRAILSIDE MUSEUMS.........................	103
X. NATIONAL PARK SERVICE AND OTHER PROJECTS...	112
XI. INDIAN SUMMER.............................	121
APPENDIX: Memorials and Resolutions, Memberships and Offices, Papers and Addresses...........................	128
INDEX...	139

List of Illustrations

Hermon Carey Bumpus............................frontispiece	
Laurin Aurelius Bumpus and Abbie Ann Eaton Bumpus....	26
Hermon Carey Bumpus and Lucy Ella Nightingale, 1886....	26

The reappearance of the "extinct" tilefish was a dramatic incident of Bumpus' Woods Hole days	33
Hermon Carey Bumpus (from the painting by Howard E. Smith in Sayles Hall, Brown University)	58
American Museum of Natural History	59
A bungalow from the Philippine exhibit at the St. Louis Exposition became the Bumpus summer home	59
The Brown Bear bonds, a Bumpus idea, brought contributions to Brown University's endowment drive	90
There were Little Brown Bear bonds, too	between 90 and 91
The trailside museum, now familiar to all national park tourists, was originated by Bumpus	between 90 and 91
The natural history shrine—another educational device conceived by Bumpus	91
Boston cartoonists had a field day when Bumpus suggested fuller labels for the trees on the Common	110
Bumpus Butte, Yellowstone National Park	122
Bumpus in Yellowstone Park, where a trailside museum will be named for him	123

HERMON CAREY BUMPUS
Yankee Naturalist

CHAPTER I

Ancestry and Boyhood

LIKE most native New Englanders Hermon Carey Bumpus was much interested in family genealogy. Through many years of careful investigation he discovered that he was of the ninth generation of the descendants of Edouard Bon Passe, a French Huguenot who came to Plymouth, Massachusetts, in 1621 as a member of the so-called Cushman Party of thirty-five persons, including "lusty young men."

Since Edouard's time the family name has undergone various changes. Edouard, like the majority of his contemporaries, could not write even his name. His mark was something like a figure eight. The French *Bon Passe*, translated into the English equivalent, means "good speed" or "good report." To write it out in English required some effort, however, and so the early recorders generally adopted their own phonetic spelling, which varied, according to the generation, from Bonpasse to Bumpas, and again from Bumpus to Bump or Bumps.

After spending some seven years in Plymouth, Edouard, or Edward, moved across the bay to Duxbury, as did many of the Pilgrims, including John Alden and Myles Standish. Here and in the neighboring towns of Rochester, the Bridgewaters, and Wareham, the family resided for the next four generations. In 1776, in the fifth generation, one Zephaniah purchased part of a tract in the Province of Maine known as Shepardsfield and subsequently incorporated into the towns of Hebron and Buckfield.

In 1862, in the town of Buckfield, Hermon Carey Bumpus,

Zephaniah's great-great-grandson, was born. Although over a century had passed since the family had first settled in the Maine wilderness, they were still living in rather primitive conditions in a rural settlement. However, Hebron Academy had been established, and Hermon's father, Laurin Aurelius Bumpus, had been in attendance there for short periods, studying Latin, English, and mathematics.

When William and Hannah Bumpus, Laurin's grandparents, set up housekeeping in what was then a part of Massachusetts, they became the neighbors and friends of other families descended from members of the Plymouth Colony, among whom were the Cushman family. Through association at church and at school the children of the two families became friends, and in due time Laurin fell in love with the lovely Nancy Cushman, three years his junior, and married her.

In order to provide for a wife Laurin decided to go into partnership with his older brother Isaac, and the firm of I. C. & L. A. Bumpus, Cabinet Makers, was formed in 1856 at Buckfield. The two young men spent long, hard hours at their work, making Hitchcock chairs, which they built, painted, and delivered for the small sum of seventy-five cents each. When called upon they also built and lined coffins, for three dollars apiece.

Laurin Bumpus was a devout man and throughout his life was extremely responsive to the religious atmosphere of his time. Daily morning prayers were a habit strictly adhered to in his family, and Laurin, always of a musical nature, accompanied the singing of hymns on the small parlor organ. He took an active interest in church affairs, and in admiration for their minister, the Reverend Albion K. Small, named his first child, born July 29, 1858, Albion Cushman Bumpus. Five months later the young mother died, leaving the baby without maternal care and ending an extremely happy domestic life.

In the Sunday school class that Laurin conducted was a

ANCESTRY AND BOYHOOD

young schoolteacher named Abbie Ann Eaton, who lived on a nearby farm in East Buckfield with her father and a maternal aunt, Lucinda Lincoln. Abbie was attractive, competent, and, for those times, well educated, and was actively interested in church affairs. Laurin became much attached to her, and on October 19, 1859, they were quietly married. Their marriage, which lasted more than forty years, was a happy one.

Their first child, Hermon Carey Bumpus, was born May 5, 1862. The name Hermon was chosen because of its biblical significance, and the middle name, Carey, was that of a foreign missionary then much admired.

The following year Laurin's brother Isaac, always of a restless nature, decided to seek his fortune in Boston, and the partnership which had continued for seven years was dissolved. Laurin then opened in Buckfield an "East India and Dry Goods" general store with a local resident, C. H. Atwood, as his partner. However, Laurin was more interested in religious activities than in commerce, and the results did not always please his partner. One day while discussing church affairs with one of his customers, Laurin forgot that he had left the spigot of the molasses barrel open while filling a jug for another customer. The floor was soon flooded with the sticky mess and Atwood insisted that Laurin pay for the damage personally. Further, Laurin believed the use of tobacco to be a sin and would not permit its sale in the store, while Atwood insisted that a country store without plug tobacco was like apple pie without cheese. It is not surprising that the partnership broke up.

In 1866 Laurin moved his family to Charlestown, Massachusetts, near East Cambridge, where his brother Isaac had found employment as a cabinetmaker with the firm of Braman & Shaw. Here in Charlestown at a Sunday school gathering Hermon Carey, only five years old, gave his first public address. He later wrote about it to his uncle. The letter, which reveals the religious atmosphere in which the child lived, was painfully printed with a lead pencil in a cramped childish hand and with the weird spelling and the originality in the management of capital letters characteristic of the very young.

dear UNCLE LINCOLN
I SPoke this PIECE IN the CONCert I WANT you to write ME A lettr For ALLie got one From HIS Grand fAther ANd I WANt to have A Lettr to the Blood of Jesu Christ His soN, CleNseth US from ALL SIN thou GOd sees me Write soon The PIECE was:—

>We're glad to see you here tonight,
>And welcome you with joy,
>Each blue, and black, and grey-eyed girl,
>Each smiling little boy.
>
>Our parents too we're glad to see
>Our friends and teachers dear,
>I hope the boys will keep quite still
>So that you all may hear.
>
>I never was in all my life
>In such a scene as this,
>But I will also welcome you,
>And throw you all a kiss.

Hermon manifested early his interest in things of a biological nature. Family prayers became a sort of game for him, to see how often he could get his father to read the story of Jonah and the whale. Having pondered the matter for some time he inquired one day, "If Jonah was thrown up on dry land, did he go swimming to wash himself all clean again?"— a question prophetic of his wholesome regard for scientific exegesis.

In 1868 the family moved from Charlestown to Boston. Given Laurin's religious inclinations, it is natural that he should have become interested in the remarkable "works of faith" being performed by a prominent Boston physician, Dr. Charles Cullis. It was Dr. Cullis' belief that through prayerful intercession with the Creator, disease could be ar-

ANCESTRY AND BOYHOOD

rested, physical suffering alleviated, and ultimate cure achieved. To further his work in this direction the doctor bought a settlement house on Willard Street near the North Station in Boston, opened a mission chapel, and outfitted a so-called repository for religious literature. In 1868 he engaged Laurin Bumpus to act as his advocate and general superintendent and allotted him a few rooms on the third and fourth floors of the building as living quarters of a sort for his family.

Laurin found the work congenial to his taste, but it was difficult to support a family of four, including two growing boys, on a salary of forty dollars a month. Nor was housekeeping easy. There were no bathrooms in the house, so that all water had to be carried up, and all excreta down, three or four flights of stairs. Young Hermon is reported to have been a frail child, and his health was not improved by the unwholesome living conditions. Two successive fractures during this period made the family's physician exclaim, "Why, his bones must be made of glass!"

Realizing the urgency of a change in their way of living and determined that her husband should be able to carry on his work free from worry, Abbie took her two boys back to East Buckfield for the summer months. There they lived with their great-aunt Lucinda Lincoln and benefited from the country air and the comfortable surroundings. Abbie, satisfied that her children were cared for and happy, worked in the hop fields some three miles away to pay for their room and board.

Even at this early age Hermon's love of nature must have been marked enough to leave an impression on his greataunt's neighbors. Some fifty years later, when he took his own sons to visit the old Lincoln homestead, he met an elderly and eccentric spinster, Sarah Warren, who greeted him with a wry question, "Why, Hermon Carey Bumpus, have you come up here again looking for turtles and snakes?"

In the atmosphere of religious emotionalism that prevailed

at the time, the Cullis Mission and Repository flourished and its functions multiplied. Alleged cures through the "exercise of faith" were announced and widely accepted as fact. There were no charges for treatment, but gifts, entirely voluntary, were many. The enterprise was presumably a charity, since it was not money-making and depended upon "faith." Additional buildings on Willard Street were secured, "free-will workers" were engaged, patients were housed, and the training of missionaries was undertaken. Gifts for the project seemed to keep pace with its expansion. In 1870 an estate at Grove Hall in Dorchester, a suburb of Boston, was purchased. The main building, which had been at one time a private mansion and subsequently a hotel, was badly in need of repair, but there were also certain minor buildings, which became the "Consumptive Home."

Laurin, who had demonstrated at the Willard Street settlement his unusual ability for administrative as well as devotional projects, was placed in charge at Grove Hall and temporarily settled his family in one of the buildings known as the "Children's Home." This house was already occupied by several tuberculous children, mostly the poor offspring of the afflicted adults who occupied quarters in the larger Consumptive Home. The domestic environment was not good for his wife or for his sons, Albion and Hermon, now thirteen and nine years of age respectively, and presently Laurin fitted up one of the small houses as a residence for the family.

Shortly afterward his brother Isaac came to live with them. Since Isaac was still working at his carpenter's bench in East Cambridge, several miles distant, Abbie now had to rise in winter before daybreak to prepare breakfast, attend family prayers, and put up a lunch for Isaac, who left on the horse cars at six in order to reach the shop in Cambridge by seven. All this was quite naturally a heavy tax upon Abbie's Christian fortitude, but she did not complain.

A score of young people of both sexes occupied Dr. Cullis'

Children's Home, there were perhaps sixty patients in the larger hospital, and an addition was in process of construction. A church was built, a Deaconess House was constructed, revivals were organized, Sunday schools were established, and a large estate in Walpole was purchased to be used as a "Cancer Home." In Boston itself quarters were engaged on West Street, and valuable property was acquired on Beacon Hill near the State House. Here midday meetings of a highly emotional character were held, at which not only money but also watches and jewelry of various kinds were eagerly thrown into the contribution boxes by the repentant devotees.

Laurin had done a wonderful job. In addition to supervising the activities in the city, he had planned and directed the erection of buildings at Grove Hall. He operated the farm, saw that the cattle were provided for, engaged the kitchen servants, and took measures to see that the patients were well fed. His numerous activities also included administering prayers to the sick and dying, and from his scanty salary he often purchased furnishings to brighten the drab coffins supplied by the "Overseers of the Poor." If a minister failed to appear at some last rite, Laurin modestly took charge. He could also substitute for an absent organist.

However, as the expansion of the project eventually began to exceed donations, bills kept coming in that could not be met. This worried Laurin. Butchers and grocers seemed to be losing their faith in "faith," and Abbie too began to detect flaws in the fervency of the promoter, Dr. Cullis. Living on the grounds of an institution also presented many difficulties. Accordingly, in May of 1877 Laurin purchased a small home on Wayne Street in Boston Highlands, near the institution, and there he took his little family, along with his brother Isaac. Two years later, in May 1879, he terminated his work with Dr. Cullis, and in the following November he became pastor's assistant to Dr. Cephas B. Crane of the Shawmut Avenue Baptist Church. There he remained for two years, until November 1881, building up the membership and receiving the approbation and sympathetic cooperation of both the pastor and the officers of the organization.

While living at Boston Highlands Hermon went over to Squantum one winter day in 1877 to hunt for shore birds. Instead of taking the long hike by way of Quincy he ventured to cross the Neponset River on the ice. While he was over the channel the ice gave way and he went through. Thinking only of his precious gun, he threw it forward on the ice and thus gave himself sufficient bearing surface to climb out on. After he had walked the two miles home his mother had to immerse him in a bathtub of warm water to thaw out his clothes so they could be removed. The fact that he could withstand such exposure must have made his mother feel that the hours she had spent in the hop fields of Maine were not in vain.

As a result of the family's various moves Hermon attended a number of different schools: the Poplar Street Primary School in Boston's North End in 1868, the Winthrop Street Primary School in Roxbury in 1871, the Dale Street Grammar School in Roxbury in 1873, and the Gibson School in Dorchester in 1877. In his class at Gibson School was Childe Hassam, the painter, for whom, Dr. Bumpus confessed in later life, he occasionally filched artists' paints from the school studio. The principal at that time was William E. Endicott, one of the ablest headmasters of the Boston school system, an inspiring teacher and a man of strong character. At graduation time in 1878 Hermon submitted an essay on frogs which Mr. Endicott, recognizing its merit and promise, asked him to read at the graduation exercises. Bashfulness made Hermon refuse, and a girl classmate had to read it for him.

Coming to the fore at this time, along with his interest in biology, was Hermon's other dominant interest, practical education. Although he had hesitated to appear on the school rostrum at graduation, he had no inhibitions about breaking into print, for he wrote the following letter to the editor of the local paper.

Boston Highlands,
July 7, 1875.

MR. EDITOR:

As I was strolling through a neighbor's pasture today, I noticed that a horse was hobbled by putting a strap on the left forward foot and on the right hind foot, and by walking had got it caught between the hoof and shoe on the right hind foot, giving but little chance to move. The place where the horse stood looked as though he had been standing there a number of days having almost starved for want of food. By the assistance of a boy who was with me and a jack knife we released the poor animal from its pittiable condition. The strap which was round one of his hind legs had wore through the flesh near the bone. When the horse realized it was liberated it showed its gratitude by giving several kicks. Please give information through your valible paper in regard to the best method of hobbleing a horse. If you consider this worthy, please insert.

Respectfully,
H. C. BUMPUS

At thirteen years of age Hermon wanted people to know how to hobble horses. Throughout his life as an educator it was always the practical thing he wanted people to know. To know the names of the flowers, plants, and birds one saw and to know something of the geology of the terrain where one lived seemed to him far more important than to know the French subjunctives or to be able to read Greek and Latin. This attitude was to bring him in later years into more than one academic battle, but he always felt such battles worth the trouble if they resulted in some liberalization of education and educational methods.

His originality in presenting ideas and objects, which was to make his museum work so successful, was also noticeable at this time. Among the boys of all New England towns it was then the custom to dress up in grotesque costumes and take part in the "Antiques and Horribles" parade which was as much a part of the Fourth of July celebration as were the fireworks and crackers. At this time the "Negro Exodus" was causing much public interest, for thousands of Negroes were reported leaving the South for Kansas and other midwestern states. Hermon got his friends to dress up as southern Negroes and the youthful group won the prize for the most original idea in costume.

After his graduation from the Gibson School he entered the Dorchester High School, where he became a close friend of Mart Wilder. Mart's father, Marshall P. Wilder, was president of the Massachusetts Horticultural Society, and his estate was not far from the Cullis Consumptive Home. On his grounds were extensive greenhouses—one of the standard red roses of commerce today bears his name—and in his home a large library. Access to a good private library was a novelty to young Hermon, and he was not slow in making the most of such an opportunity. From this time on he was to be found at the Wilders' home far more frequently than at the Consumptive Home.

Under the influence of the Wilders Hermon's interest in animals was extended to plants, and for the rest of his life horticulture was one of his greatest joys. When later, as director of the American Museum of Natural History, he felt his income sufficient to build a small greenhouse, he confessed that one of his life ambitions had been realized. It is little wonder that during his younger professional years he enjoyed teaching courses in botany on more than one occasion.

In the extensive grounds of the Wilder estate and the Consumptive Home, Hermon and Mart played "relievo," a game known to later generations as hide-and-seek. On weekends the boys went gunning together at Ponkapog, a ten-mile tramp each way, but there were few times that the young naturalists failed to return with specimens for their growing collections.

Years later Hermon's son, then in his teens, was taken by his grandmother up into the belfry of the Second Congregational Church in Dorchester to see the Paul Revere bell and also, stored there, the many birdskins and mounted specimens that his father had collected and prepared. Abbie had treasured them all those years, and until her death they were among her most precious possessions. To the ambitious little schoolteacher of Buckfield, Maine, nothing was more sacred than the collections made in his youth by Hermon, who was now director of the greatest natural history museum in the country.

His boyhood collections were not confined to birds, but included also insects and snakes, and with both his lifelong joy in practical jokes found expression. Once at evening service at the Grove Hall Church he freed a jarful of June bugs, which hit the heads of the congregation and nearly broke up the service. The parishioners thought the bugs had been attracted through the open windows by the lights, and the next week the church was fitted with screens. Snakes were frequent inhabitants of Hermon's school desk, and his brother tells of the trouble it was to capture one of the poisonous variety that had escaped into the dining room at home.

In 1878 a woman missionary, a friend of the family, was attending a meeting at the Hamilton Methodist camp meeting ground. Since Hermon was considered rather frail and in need of outdoor exercise, she volunteered to take him along with her, hoping the change of scene would benefit him both physically and morally. When he arrived at the meeting grounds he at once went to work tearing to pieces the rotten stumps that dotted the grove and unearthing the hibernating snakes that had found sanctuary there. In his unreligious quest he found and destroyed more than one hundred victims. His brother Albion maintains that this remarkable count was checked and found accurate.

While the family was living in Dorchester young Hermon captured a skunk and confined it in a barrel in the back yard. Then at the romantic age, he conceived the idea of converting this unusual animal into a pet to present to his best girl.

Just as Hermon, having anaesthetized the skunk in a barrel, had completed the operation necessary to render it a desirable pet, his father appeared on the scene and unknowingly stepped on and squashed the excised scent glands. The odor of the skunk followed him all over Dorchester as he made his pastoral calls.

The skunk survived the operation and turned out to be a charming pet, and the citizens of Dorchester became accustomed to the sight of pretty Ella Nightingale seated on her veranda fondling the little black and white animal with the malodorous reputation. The novelty of the pet soon wore off, however, and Hermon called at a dime museum in Boston to tell the manager what he had. The manager offered him five dollars for the animal if he would guarantee it "void of offense," and upon delivering it Hermon received the first financial return from his natural history proclivities.

As Hermon approached graduation from high school he realized that if he was to follow his desire to become a naturalist he must have a college education. Since he was neither a good linguist nor interested in the classics, he had made a rather poor showing in the formal education of the time, and the high school principal discouraged his ambition, saying he was not suited intellectually to pursue a higher education and advising him to seek employment in the local grocery store. Fortunately the principal's daughter, Miss Alice Collar, a teacher of languages in the public schools, thought otherwise. She took a great interest in the boy naturalist and offered to tutor him in languages at her home after school hours each day. This coaching during his junior and senior years in high school was so effective that he was able to enter Brown University in the fall of 1879. Fifty years later, when in the absence of the president it fell to his lot as senior fellow of Brown University to award the advanced degrees, he was able to give the citations in the required Latin—though not without considerable trepidation.

It was largely through the influence of Professor J. W. P.

ANCESTRY AND BOYHOOD

Jenks of Brown University and Deacon Hartshorn, the latter a close friend of his father's and a member of the university corporation, that Hermon decided to enter Brown. The deacon's influence also made possible for him some relaxation of the entrance requirements. Had the examiners held steadily to the letter of the requirements it is probable that the mercantile world would have had a poor grocery clerk and the scientific world would have lost a great naturalist. During the rest of his life Hermon always favored low entrance requirements for schools of higher learning, in the belief that all students should have opportunity to prove their ability during their freshman year, which, he held, was the time to sort the wheat from the chaff.

After Hermon entered Brown his father designed and built a comfortable home on Wayne Street in Dorchester, and the family moved in on July 3, 1882. During Hermon's sophomore year his room in the new house was occupied by a Massachusetts Institute of Technology student, George E. Hale, who endeared himself to all the family. In later years Hale became an eminent astronomer, and it was through his endeavors that the Mount Wilson Observatory was built in Pasadena, California, and that Mr. Huntington was persuaded to make his famous library a research institution. Now that World War II is over, the 200-inch telescope is to be mounted at Palomar as a supreme tribute to Hale, one of America's great scientists.

Throughout the rest of his life Hermon's father continued to carry on his philanthropic activities, giving help to the poor and establishing and maintaining neighborhood meetings, of which at least one, at Field's Corner, matured into a church organization. He also organized field days for the young people of these communities. His services at funerals were frequently requested by families who were without religious affiliations, and in the church, at both the beginning and the end of the services, he was present with words of comfort and cheer. As city missionary for the Dorchester district of Boston he held a position analogous to that of our present social service workers. He organized and conducted a Bible class that for years after his death continued to bear his name.

When Laurin died suddenly of heart disease in 1902, at Dr. Bumpus' home in New Rochelle, his wife Abbie never recovered from the shock. Before a month had passed, her body found its permanent resting place beside her beloved companion of forty-three years.

CHAPTER II

As Student and Beginning Teacher

HERMON entered Brown University in the autumn of 1879. He was assigned Room 46 in old University Hall, which had served as barracks for Rochambeau's troops during the Revolutionary War. President Robinson had spoken vigorously of the shocking condition of University Hall. "Its battered doors, its defaced walls, the gaping flooring of its hallways, and the inescapable odor of decay pervading the building" proclaimed its needs, and both within and without it was "an eyesore and a reproach."

When students living in the hall wished to build a fire it was common practice to knock more plaster from the gaping holes and tear off the laths beneath for use as kindling. The entries and doorways of the building had never been lighted at night; the students groped their way up and down as best they could. The stairways were made of hewn logs, which had become so worn in over a century of traffic that the center was substantially an inclined plane from one story to the next, enabling the students to indulge in quick descent. The floors of the rooms were so uneven that it was not unusual for a heavy piece of furniture, such as a bed, to slide from one side to the other during the night. In January of Hermon's sophomore year a smoldering fire between the ceiling of one of the classrooms and the floor above gave enthusiastic students an opportunity to do greater damage with their axes than was done by the fire itself. Eventually, in 1883, the building was remodeled.

However, matters of bodily comfort, whether of living quarters or of food, were not especially interesting to Hermon

Bumpus. Food was something to keep him nourished, and his early training had made him unmindful of privations. When he applied at a boardinghouse the proprietress, Mrs. Whitman, asked, "Do you smoke?" He replied with his most engaging smile, "No, but I can if you want me to." His attractive personality captivated those he met, and few ever forgot the experience of knowing him.

To study with men interested in the natural sciences was his greatest ambition, and he was able to realize it at Brown. In 1871 John Whipple Potter Jenks had come to Brown at the invitation of President Alexis Caswell, one of the founders of the National Academy of Sciences, to establish a museum through which the biotheological doctrine of Agassiz could be taught. An excerpt from the *Brunonian* of April 1870 shows that the ground was well prepared for him: "A cabinet of Comparative Anatomy is essential to any college. Every plant and animal is an expressed thought of God and cannot be presented through the medium of a professor." Professor Bronson, in his history of Brown University, observed: "Those thoughts of God for whom professors are no substitute were soon to be supplied." Within the year several thousand specimens of notable variety were acquired for the museum through the initiative of Professor Jenks.

At this time Brown University was undergoing a decided liberalization in curriculum. Ezekiel Gillman Robinson, who was educated for the ministry and for several years had been president of a theological school, had become president in 1872. Amazingly enough, he declared that he felt quite stifled and cramped for buildings at Brown and ashamed of the narrow range of studies, particularly in the natural sciences and modern languages. He proceeded to enlarge Rhode Island Hall and followed with the construction of a new library and a dormitory called Slater Hall after its donor. The campus was landscaped, University Hall was renovated, and the university endowment was increased from six hundred thousand dollars to one million dollars.

AS STUDENT AND BEGINNING TEACHER

Certainly no one but a man of broad vision could have achieved the conditions he brought about in the natural science faculty. While the venerable Professor Jenks was filling the newly acquired exhibition cases in Rhode Island Hall with flora and fauna shipped from Asia, Africa, and the South Seas by Baptist missionaries, President Robinson brought to the university the scholarly Dr. Alpheus Spring Packard, a distinguished advocate of the theory of evolution, to occupy an independent chair in the same field.

In view of President Robinson's early training and his long association with conservative theologians his attitude was remarkable. "Physical science some day will undoubtedly smash some of our crockery gods," he said, in one of his hearty epigrams. He was an austere old Roman and kept careful tab on both students and faculty. One day Hermon was called into his presence. He entered with fear, for owing to his love of practical jokes he was not above suspicion. Said the president, glaring at him: "You have a gun in your room!" "Yes," guiltily answered young Bumpus. "Well, the pigeons are making a mess in front of Manning Hall.... You may go." The president was not a man to waste words.

Professor Packard was Bumpus' ideal. He was, so to speak, born to the academic manner. His father was a distinguished professor of Latin and Greek, his mother the daughter of a college president. How closely his cultured tastes and inclinations resembled those of the young Bumpus is best shown by an extract from Packard's youthful diary. "I have read a good deal today in my Naturalist library. Oh, that I could wander around the earth, and collect specimens of Natural History. It seems to me that if I could know all about botany, mineralogy, geology, and conchology, and also know how to stuff birds and animals, preserve insects, and collect shells of various kinds, well, nothing could be more pleasant provided I had the finances."

The influence of Darwin and the inductive sciences was unmistakable on those who called themselves naturalists.

The period was one of variety and change. The classification of plants and animals into genera was still an alluring occupation, and the discovery, description, and naming of new species arrested the attention of botanists and geologists alike. Professor Jenks, representing as it were the end of an epoch, clung tenaciously to the ideals of the philosophy of special creation, but Packard, though a student of Agassiz, was among the leading Lamarckians. Bumpus took all the courses from Professor Packard that the catalogue offered.

Hermon was well aware that he could not continue in the congenial surroundings of Brown unless he had the necessary funds. In his search for remunerative work his early training in sketching animals and mounting specimens served him well. He was appointed an assistant in the museum and spent all his available spare time assisting Professor Jenks with the preparation of specimens. He was able also to help in the revision and illustration of many of Jenks's scientific writings. In revising one of his books on zoology, Jenks particularly cautioned his assistant to retain his statement on the use of the hippopotamus: "It is exactly fitted to dredge the rivers and keep open the channels, so apt to become filled with luxuriant growth of that tropical region known as Africa." The whimsical Bumpus countered with the query, "Shall I say the beaver was exactly fitted to dam up the rivers of North America?"

In his senior year Bumpus wrote the chapter on "Reptiles of the World" for the encyclopedia *Standard Natural History*, edited by Kingsley. More than half a century later, while visiting his youngest grandson, Frank, at Deerfield Academy, Dr. Bumpus proudly took from the library shelves a volume on natural history and showed his grandson some of the illustrations he had made to finance his college career.

However, it was not all work and no play for Bumpus. He enjoyed college life and indulged in a number of extracurricular activities. He was among those who earned the doubtful distinction of placing the numerals of the class of

AS STUDENT AND BEGINNING TEACHER

'84 high on the chapel walls. In his sophomore year he was invited to join the Delta Phi fraternity. Among his classmates he became known as the fellow who had shot, skinned, stuffed, and eaten every living animal. A picture that hung for many years in the Brown Union showed him at bow oar on the varsity crew, and the '84 classbook, *Liber Bruensis*, lists him as one of its editors. In the spring of his senior year his classmates elected him chairman of their class day committee.

In this stimulating atmosphere of scientific change and learning and college companionship the years passed quickly. Following his graduation in 1884 Bumpus spent the summer in Annisquam, the pleasant resort on Cape Ann, near Gloucester, studying in the biological laboratory recently opened by Alpheus Hyatt, then in the fall returned to Brown to continue his graduate studies. The following year he was asked to take over Professor Packard's classes while the professor was on leave. In addition he found time to prepare the Rhode Island Exhibit for the Cotton Centennial, take it to New Orleans, and set it up.

In the meantime Olivet College in Michigan had decided to establish a department of biology and offered Bumpus the professorship. He accepted their offer and went to his new post in the autumn of 1886.

Within a few months after his arrival, Professor Bumpus had collected material for a functioning zoological laboratory, though no funds for the purpose had been made available at the start. Throughout his life he held to the opinion that if, even on a small scale, one could demonstrate a project to be worth while, the financial support for its maintenance would be forthcoming. In other words, he was a strong believer that help comes to those who help themselves.

While Professor Bumpus was in New England on vacation during his second year at Olivet, he happened to read in the papers that a whale had come ashore near Provincetown. At once he went to Provincetown, secured the whale's head, cleaned off the soft parts—a prodigious and malodorous job —and shipped the skull and jawbones back to Olivet.

At Olivet too Professor Bumpus undertook some research into the embryonic development of the common garter snake, *Eutaenia*, and he experienced some difficulty in obtaining enough live female specimens for the purpose. After he had advertised in the local paper that he would give ten cents for each live specimen brought to him, the small boys of the neighborhood turned in a few snakes, but they did not come in fast enough to suit the impatient professor. Then one morning an old tramp who looked as if he knew all about the delirium tremens variety of snakes was discovered waiting on the doorstep of the laboratory. He wanted to know whether the ten-cent offer in the paper was really true and, if so, how many snakes were wanted. Dr. Bumpus dismissed him with the assurance that the offer was genuine and that the sky was the limit as to number. The next morning the old fellow turned up with a gunny sack in which there were so many squirming captives that the professor's meager salary was threatened in squaring the account.

The male snakes, which were useless in the study, were tossed through the open window of the laboratory. When the neighborhood boys discovered this, there was a return movement up the stairs of these discarded males, held in the grasp of excited youngsters seeking to claim the reward. But it did not take the professor long to recognize these repeaters, and their subsequent slaughter put an end both to their travels and to the march of dimes.

Multiplying activities prevented the writing and publication of the traditional scientific paper recording Bumpus' excursion into the development of garter snakes. He was always more concerned with doing a piece of scientific research than in preserving the results in print. Some years later, however, *Eutaenia* eggs carefully preserved in alcohol from the Olivet days served in the preparation of at least one master's thesis at Brown University.

Many years later James L. Kellogg, who had been a stu-

AS STUDENT AND BEGINNING TEACHER

dent in Professor Bumpus' first class at Olivet and was afterward professor of biology at Williams College, wrote: "I have never seen an instructor arouse in his pupils so enthusiastic an interest in himself or his subject matter. More than any other person I ever knew, he is a man of enthusiasm and unceasing energy, and I doubt if ever there was one with less bluster or selfishness about him. He is an entire stranger to anything dictatorial, and his tact in a difficult situation has always excited the wonder and admiration of his friends. He possesses a rare power of pleasing. I once heard a college president say, after a ten-minute conversation with him, that he had never met a more charming man."

In the winter of 1886 Professor Bumpus returned to the East during the Christmas holidays to marry, on December 28, Lucy Ella Nightingale, the sweetheart of his boyhood days in Dorchester. For some years her room in her father's home had been filled with young Bumpus' efforts in taxidermy. Various stuffed birds and even a pet skunk were mute testimony to the love of a naturalist.

While the couple were out driving one afternoon not long after their return to Olivet, the bride saw in a farmer's yard a gorgeous peacock with spread tail, and expressed a desire to own it. Her surprise was mingled with consternation when some time later her husband presented her with a *stuffed* peacock. However, she concealed her dismay and dutifully placed the stuffed bird in a conspicuous position on top of the upright piano, a place it retained as the family moved from house to house through many years.

When their first child, Hermon Carey, Jr., had reached the crawling stage, fear of his falling down the stairs was uppermost in his parents' thoughts. Instead of building the usual unsightly gate, however, they discovered that the same purpose was served by placing at the head of the stairs one of their stuffed birds, a great horned owl with staring yellow eyes and curved beak. From this apparition small Hermon Carey kept his distance.

In 1888 Clark University was founded at Worcester,

Massachusetts. Its first president, Dr. G. Stanley Hall, had brought from Johns Hopkins University the ideals of scientific scholarship for which that institution was so well known, and had assembled about him a notable group of scholars in biology—Whitman, Donaldson, Mall, Bauer, Watase, McMerrick, and Wheeler among them—men who without exception were to become outstanding members of the scientific world in their chosen fields.

Bumpus succumbed to the temptation to study with such outstanding American and European scholars in the informal and close association of professors and students. After three years as a teacher at Olivet he returned to New England in 1889 with his wife and young son to accept a fellowship of six hundred dollars at Clark University, with the purpose of completing his work for the doctor's degree. He had previously spent two years in graduate study at Brown, and accordingly the following year, with the presentation of a notable thesis on the American lobster, he was granted the degree of Doctor of Philosophy. For the remainder of his life he had the satisfaction of being the recipient of the first Ph.D. degree from Clark University, and for many years he was its oldest living alumnus.

CHAPTER III

Woods Hole

IN THE same year that Clark University was founded, 1888, the Marine Biological Laboratory was opened at Woods Hole, Massachusetts. It was patterned after the marine station founded in 1872 by Dr. Anton Dohrn at Naples, where biologists from all over the world forgathered, as in an international university.

The Marine Biological Laboratory had been conceived originally as a graduate institution where biologists could continue their research work during the summer months under the nominal directorship of Charles Otis Whitman. In 1889, however, with the approval of the director, Dr. Bumpus undertook to develop and maintain at the laboratory a summer training school for the initiation of young candidates into the biological ranks. So popular and effective did this innovation become that he was made assistant director of the laboratory. He was only thirty years of age at the time, as Dr. Frank R. Lillie points out in an account of the Woods Hole institution.* This position he held until 1895, when he accepted the directorship of the U.S. Bureau of Fisheries laboratories, also at Woods Hole.

A chain of the Elizabeth Islands, which separates Buzzard's Bay from Vineyard Sound, extends out from Woods Hole toward the southwest. The outermost of these islands is Penikese, across the bay from the old whaling city of New Bedford. Because of its easy access from New Bedford, then

* *The Woods Hole Marine Biological Laboratory.* Chicago: University of Chicago Press, 1944, p. 119.

an active port, Louis Agassiz in 1873 had set up on Penikese the first marine laboratory in America. The laboratory was abandoned after Agassiz's death, but the idea persisted and the Penikese laboratory is remembered today as the progenitor of many marine stations for the study of biology on both the Atlantic and Pacific coasts. Remains of the old laboratory were still discernible when the Marine Biological Laboratory at Woods Hole was founded, and both students and teachers not infrequently made expeditions to the island. On one such expedition Bumpus found Agassiz's famous dictum, "Study Nature not Books," written in crayon on a sheet of brown paper by Agassiz himself. This souvenir found sanctuary on the walls of the main building at Woods Hole, which in a sense had arisen from the ashes of Penikese.

The M.B.L., as it is known to its members, became the spiritual descendant and legatee of the former laboratories at Penikese and Annisquam. From the start it has been the mecca of American biologists, who each summer gather there from all parts of the country to pursue their investigations in favorable surroundings.

Throughout his life Dr. Bumpus retained an active interest in the progress of the Marine Biological Laboratory. He was a member of the board of trustees from 1897 to 1942 and made it a point to attend all meetings. During its early years the laboratory, like many another scientific institution, was short of funds. To overcome this handicap Dr. Bumpus conceived the idea that the laboratory could act as a supply depot from which colleges and high schools giving courses in the increasingly popular natural sciences could obtain biological specimens.

Since Woods Hole is situated near the confluence of the Labrador Current and the Gulf Stream, it is possible to collect from the waters there marine flora and fauna peculiar to both Arctic and tropical waters. It is said that this can be done in only one other location in the world.

To collect the specimens for the commercial supply department the services of George M. Gray, a "natural naturalist,"

Laurin Aurelius Bumpus and
Abbie Ann Eaton Bumpus

Hermon Carey Bumpus and Lucy Ella Nightingale, 1886

were obtained. For several years before this appointment Mr. Gray had been a skilled taxidermist in Providence, and at the same time had worked at Brown University, looking after the more practical side of the domestic economy of the biology department. By a series of promotions he became in time the head of the supply department of the Marine Biological Laboratory. The yearly income from the supply department often ran into five figures and was an important factor in seeing the institution through some serious financial crises. In his capacity as head of the staff of collectors Gray served a larger number of students and research workers in biology than any other man anywhere at any time.

In the summer of 1896, instead of returning as usual to the Marine Biological Laboratory, Dr. Bumpus spent the vacation months investigating the skeletal structure of *Necturus*, a genus of salamanders, with the X-ray.

A considerably larger field in which to exercise his genius for organization came to him in 1897, when Commissioner Marshall McDonald appointed him director of the scientific work of the U.S. Bureau of Fisheries, the laboratory of which was located at Woods Hole, just across the way from the Marine Biological Laboratory. Here Spencer Fullerton Baird, the founder, had hoped that scientists could make practical application to human welfare of their research in marine life, and Dr. Bumpus set out to realize this purpose.

The government station at Woods Hole had for some time been out of congressional favor. At the time Dr. Bumpus became director the plant had so deteriorated that it was all but useless. The scientific equipment had been destroyed, and while the buildings were unoccupied the wharves and basins had reached a stage of picturesque but ruinous disintegration. The vessels of the Fish Commission were seldom seen.

Nevertheless, Dr. Bumpus saw the possibility of making the place a great biological center. Thinking over the problem, he decided that if the laboratory was to succeed, it must be made to appeal to the taxpayer in a practical manner, and he thought this purpose could be achieved by turning its investigations into channels that would solve such practical economic problems as the rehabilitation of the lobster industry. In a short time he had forty scientists at work.

In keeping with the ideals of Baird, the larger craft of the Fish Commission—including the *Fish Hawk* with a crew of forty, the *Grampus*, a large two-masted schooner of the Gloucester type, the *Phalarope*, a converted steam yacht, and the *Blue Wing*, a small tugboat—were placed in commission and put at the service of the scientific director and his staff. The *Blue Wing* was used for towing whale boats, which were often filled with the scientific staff—described by the townspeople as "bug hunters"—on their collecting trips in waters adjacent to Woods Hole.

The *Fish Hawk* offered a considerable problem, for though it was under the administration of the Fish Commission its crew was composed of U.S. Navy personnel. This unusual arrangement resulted when the Fish Commission lent the boat to the Navy for the blockade of Santiago Harbor during the Spanish-American War. It is not hard to imagine with what lack of enthusiasm the officers of the U.S. Navy took their orders from the director of the Fish Commission and with what contempt they regarded the "bug hunters." Difficult situations arose in which Dr. Bumpus' tact and powers of persuasion were taxed to the utmost, for the captain of the *Fish Hawk* often found it convenient to offer excuses for not carrying out the voyages into surrounding waters. However, Dr. Bumpus' personality was one that even a hardened naval officer could not resist for long, and on many occasions the *Fish Hawk*'s dredge brought up from the ocean floor flora and fauna that were much appreciated by the scientists at the station.

In an address on "The Importance of Extended Scientific Investigation," given before the National Fisheries Congress and published in the *Bulletin* of the Fish Commission for 1897, Bumpus clarified his proposed program and gave some idea of his vision for the future.

"We meet here as members of a government that within less than three decades has not only revolutionized the methods of fish culture, but has preserved to its several States, inland as well as seaboard, an industry yielding an annual income of over $45,000,000; a government which now maintains for the propagation of its fishes a fleet of steam and sailing vessels, more than a score of liberally equipped hatching and breeding stations, and which gratuitously issues to those unable to inspect its work a series of publications of great value to practical fishermen, of vast importance to the fish culturist, and of sterling worth to the scientific world. The names of Baird, Verrill, Goode, and Ryder are familiar in every college and university, and their well-worn publications are conspicuous in biological laboratories from Italy to Scandinavia and from Liverpool to Tokyo.

"The United States Fish Commission is responsible for the $2,000,000 annual shad industry, and for the successful planting of cod fry upon the coast of New England whereby eastern waters have been replenished. The migrations of the menhaden have been explained by the researches of Dr. Peck, and Professor Libbey has clarified the important question of the distribution of the mackerel, but other problems remain to be solved.

"For some years the starfish have wrought havoc among the oysters of the cold waters of our coast. The fishermen have laboriously mopped the beds with tangles of cotton waste, but have remained quite ignorant of the life habits of their enemy. A scientific study of the subject by A. D. Mead, however, has revealed many facts which point towards a possible, if not probable, early correction of the evil.

"We should be careful, however, lest the consciousness of a successful past act as a sedative for the present. The lines of research, wisely indicated by the founders of American fish culture, should be assiduously followed, and the by-paths explored."

Dr. Bumpus went on to outline a practical program for

the development of the market for food fish, a program which should have in mind much needed improvement in methods of preparing, packing, shipping, storing, and retailing fish. Finally, he urged the importance of providing such instruction in practical fishery as was already established in schools in Norway, Sweden, Germany, and Japan; for, although there were in our country over a million men, women, and children dependent upon the fisheries for their existence, there was no school, academy, or college in the entire United States which gave even one short course in the economics of fish culture.

He concluded his survey of future possibilities with a plea for renewed activity in biological research in which the practical and the scientific could be combined and coordinated, at such a station as that at Woods Hole, in instruction and research.

During his connection with the Fish Commission Dr. Bumpus not only stimulated a revival of activity at the Woods Hole station but also produced three papers recording personal investigations.

The first of these papers concerned the fate of the flatfish fry liberated along the coast. To determine whether the liberated fry hatched at the station were the ones that grew to maturity and accounted for the increased catch of the fishermen, Dr. Bumpus employed a biometric technique. The spines of the dorsal fins of flatfish vary in number, and the local population of a species shows a characteristic variability curve with respect to the number of dorsal spines, a number that remains constant throughout life. By determining the curve for the liberated fry and comparing it with that of the captured adult fish, Dr. Bumpus hoped to discover whether the adult fish were the ones reared in the hatchery. Although the results were not as conclusive as he had hoped, the conception and execution of the idea were certainly ingenious.

His second paper dealt with the peregrinations of lobsters.

It is illegal to sell lobsters with eggs except to the U.S. Fish Commission, which strips off the eggs and hatches them artificially in order to protect the fry during the critical period of their development; for when they are free and swimming these little creatures are the choicest of food for all fishes. After the brood lobsters have been stripped of their eggs they are liberated, and Dr. Bumpus wanted to find out how far and in what direction these brood lobsters traveled. Copper identification tags, bearing numbers and the request that they be returned to the Fish Commission, were attached to the rostrums of about five hundred specimens, which were then liberated in recorded localities during June and July of 1898.

Although many lobstermen doubtless did not bother to return the tags as requested and other tags were probably lost accidentally or as a consequence of molting, nevertheless a sufficient number were returned to make it evident that the lobsters had little chance of dying outside a fisherman's pot. An instructive map was made showing the direction and distance these wandering wards of Uncle Sam had gone and the time involved in their migratory travels. The lobsters drifted or kicked themselves as far as twelve to sixteen miles from the point of their liberation—even as far as Cuttyhunk and Gay Head—before they were caught a second time.

The lobster lover owes a great deal to Dr. Bumpus and his associate, Dr. A. D. Mead. Dr. Bumpus, who had written his doctoral thesis on the embryology of the lobster, perceived the importance of keeping the lobsterlings in captivity until they were old enough to drop to the bottom and escape the attention of their enemies by hiding between the rocks. It had formerly been necessary to turn them loose as soon as they were hatched or they would devour one another in such numbers that it seemed hardly worth while to hatch them. But turning them adrift was worse than keeping them in captivity, for at that age they floated on the water and were easily taken by their numerous enemies.

To solve this problem Dr. Bumpus and Dr. Mead constructed cloth basins in which large paddles, like revolving fans, kept the water constantly stirred. Provided with ample food, the lobsterlings were kept alive until they were old enough to escape their would-be devourers. This device was an important factor in rehabilitating the lobster industry.

Dr. Bumpus' third paper told a most exciting story—the rediscovery, at the edge of the continental shelf off the eastern coast of southern New England, of great numbers of tilefish, *Lopholatilus chamaeleonticeps*, which had not been seen since 1879, when they were reported off Nantucket. The newspapers gave the following account:

"In March and April, 1882, vessels entering New York and other Atlantic ports reported that they passed through countless numbers of dead fish while crossing the northern edge of the Gulf Stream. Investigation proved that they were tilefish and that they appeared on the surface of the water over an area of 170 miles in length and 25 miles in width. A conservative estimate placed their number at upwards of 1,438,720,000, and allowing ten pounds to each fish, there would have been 288 pounds of fish for every man, woman, and child in the U.S."

In the years 1884, 1885, and 1886 the U.S. Fish Commission boat *Albatross* dredged over the "tilefish grounds" for 128 official hauls without obtaining a single specimen of the tilefish, which was therefore supposed to be extinct. However, in February 1897 the 78-ton schooner *Mabel Kenniston* was overtaken by a gale off Georges Bank and blown westward about 120 miles, to a position about 140 miles southwest of No Man's Land. The captain set haddock trawls and caught thirty tilefish weighing six to fifteen pounds each. The unfamiliar fish were landed in Gloucester, where they were distributed, and those who ate them pronounced them "better than salmon."

Dr. Bumpus had not heard of the catch made by the *Mabel Kenniston*, but he did know of the supposed extinction

The reappearance of the "extinct" tilefish was a dramatic incident of Bumpus' Woods Hole days

of the tilefish, thought by many to be due to a shift in the Gulf Stream, and he was curious to learn whether any had survived. In August 1898 he ordered the two-masted Gloucester-type schooner *Grampus* placed in commission for the presumed purpose of examining the surface fauna of the warmer waters of the Gulf Stream. Captain Bob Veeder was a bit surprised when the doctor told him to take along some old trawls from the garret of the station, as well as a few barrels of menhaden bait. This seemed queer equipment for investigation of surface fauna, but the captain knew the doctor's reputation for doing the unusual, and so asked no questions.

At noon on August 13 a trawl was set in seventy fathoms of water in latitude 40° 11′ N and longitude 70° 48′ W. After it had been on the bottom not more than an hour it was drawn in. Eight tilefish had been taken. The capture of these tilefish was just what Dr. Bumpus had hoped for, but he had not dared to tell anyone about it and the capture was a great surprise to those on board the boat.

After returning to Woods Hole for better equipment the *Grampus* returned to the same locality later in August and set the trawls in seventy-five fathoms. Dr. Bumpus writes of the results: "After remaining out for a few hours the trawls were hauled and from the deck of the *Grampus* we could see the sailors tugging at the line and rolling the great fish into the boat. When the dory came alongside the men drew forty-seven beautiful tilefish on the deck!" The record for the entire day's fishing was seventy-three, and the following day seventy-eight more were added before the bait was exhausted. The *Grampus* then headed for Montauk Point to distribute the catch to the soldiers at Camp Wickoff. They arrived there while Theodore Roosevelt was visiting the camp, and Dr. Bumpus had a tilefish cooked for the famous Rough Rider's dinner.

The human story of this memorable voyage is recalled by Dr. A. D. Mead, who was one of the party that discovered this new food supply. They were fogbound and seasick the night of their return trip, but Captain Bob Veeder, with the skill and instinct of a true navigator, piloted the *Grampus* safely along an unseen course and arrived precisely at the dock at Montauk Point. They unloaded their fishy cargo, weighing a thousand pounds, at the hospital, thanks to General Joe Wheeler, whose prompt disposal of entangling red tape made possible the welcome gift to the Spanish-American War veterans stationed at Camp Wickoff.

Since that time tilefish have appeared in Atlantic markets as one of our standard food fishes, but speculation as to the cause of the disappearance of the tilefish in 1882 and the reason for its return still occupies the puzzled scientists.

Largely because of his work at the Woods Hole station, Dr. Bumpus was elected president of the International Fisheries Congress at its fourth meeting, held in Washington in 1908.

CHAPTER IV

Brown University, 1890-1900

IN HIS first address to the governing body of Brown University, President E. Benjamin Andrews, who succeeded Ezekiel Robinson as president of the university, gave evidence of his progressive educational policies. It was his opinion that the establishment of graduate work at Brown would have a favorable effect upon both the undergraduate teaching at the university and the intellectual atmosphere of the campus. "Nothing in the world would so inspire our undergraduates," he said, "as the presence on these grounds of a few score of graduate students, pursuing and discussing their advanced studies and conducting special research in our library and laboratories. Nothing else could so spur our faculty to that enterprise which is imperative as to have to direct and examine investigations in these higher fields."

In the autumn of 1890 President Andrews summoned Dr. Bumpus from Woods Hole and specifically commissioned him to put these policies into effect in relation to biology. By virtue of his baptism at Brown and his immersion in the atmosphere of Clark University and the Marine Biological Laboratory, Dr. Bumpus was considered "exactly fitted to carry out this commission."

Dr. Bumpus was twenty-eight years old when he became a professor at his alma mater. At the time of his appointment President Andrews said of him: "In the opinion of the best authorities he has, of his age, no superior as a specialist in his line. He is not, however, a narrow specialist but thoroughly informed in every branch of the science of life. He is withal a stirring teacher and an affable and cultivated gentleman."

Professor Bumpus brought with him from Woods Hole, as his first graduate student, a man who was to be his closest friend throughout his life and his successor at Brown. This was Albert Davis Mead, then an inexperienced youth in whose presence one felt a faint adumbration of coming events in graduate work.

As capital to work with, Bumpus had inexhaustible energy, boundless optimism, and the hearty endorsement of the president. He needed laboratory space, equipment and apparatus, biological periodicals, and financial support to aid in the material and spiritual welfare of the graduate students working under him. All these things the university, through its president, was more than willing to provide, but it was not in a financial position to do so. However, it never occurred to Bumpus to be sorry for himself. He had a strong ally in necessity.

During all his life Professor Bumpus' love of teaching ran a close and not infrequently an even race with his interest in the natural sciences. With his coming the methods of teaching biology at Brown underwent a drastic change. The orthodox plan had been for the professor to meet his students, call the roll, ask a series of questions concerning his previous lecture and assignments, make mental notes of their proficiency or lack of it, and then dictate for the rest of the hour. Bumpus' procedure was radically different.

A group of seniors elected to take the first course he offered, in the anatomy of vertebrate animals. It proved to be a cooperative affair, in which the students not only obtained a knowledge of vertebrate anatomy but enjoyed as well the friendships formed among students and instructors. Specimens majestically installed in the museum were ruthlessly withdrawn from their alcoholic containers and used for class demonstrations. When one of the animals at the zoo in nearby Roger Williams Park died it was in the park that the class next met, in order to profit by a post-mortem examination of the strange animal.

At this time James W. Southwick was converting one of the park buildings into a natural history museum where the public might learn more about nature. Professor Bumpus at once utilized this museum as an adjunct to his teaching and derived much pleasure from assisting Mr. Southwick in the preparation of his material for exhibition.

In later years Professor Bumpus wrote of the period when the biology department at Brown was being founded: "Recognizing that one who plans to enter science as a profession should have an opportunity to discover and exercise his teaching aptitude, it was the policy of the department to encourage advanced students and especially enthusiastic ones to plan and supervise the work of others. To be perfectly frank, such duties also relieved the responsible staff from a certain amount of routine, and incidentally without adding to the budget. In any event it seemed to add to the joy of the temporary incumbent and the callow members of the class were slow in discovering the so-called 'guinea-pig' factor."

One of his first students, Herbert Eugene Walter, later professor of biology at Brown, writes of Dr. Bumpus in these early years: "There was nothing cut and dried about Professor Bumpus's teaching. Here he showed his originality. While he modestly declares it was due to his laziness, those who sat under his rostrum speak of it as one of the elements of his success that he did not bring into the classroom a lot of models elaborately prepared in advance, but when he wanted to demonstrate some process would grab up someone's soft hat or pull out a handkerchief and skillfully wind it in his hands to show the changes in form from one stage in the development of the mollusk to the other.

"Professor Bumpus collected under his wing a squad of young disciples whom he immediately put to work studying invertebrates. I do not recall much about any lectures, textbooks, or educational devices, for which he had little use, but I do recall that we found ourselves willingly working long hours, studying specimens of all sorts at first hand and ranging through the entire library in pursuit of aid and information as we needed it, while Bumpus was everywhere helping us to help ourselves.

"I do not even recall that we were given tests or examinations, but I *do* remember that we acquired a speaking acquaintance with the animal kingdom. During the third term we turned our attention, by special request, rather than by catalogue sanction, to embryology, after the same pioneer method.

"Dr. Bumpus's catholic method was to suggest projects and leave a free hand to others for the working out of details. Thus in my diary I find the following entries.

Sept. 29, 1892. Last night at 8 o'clock Dr. Bumpus came in our room with the fresh head of a big tortoise which we tackled for skull and brain until 11 P.M., when he returned and said, 'Come on, boys, let's go and have some ice cream. You have worked long enough.' An unusual college professor, I do confess. He even suggested that we have a smoke if we cared to. He surely is a jewel treating us as his equals. Tomorrow we will finish up the tortoise head. We got out the brain *in toto*, with long enough cranial nerve stubs to show in good shape, and now it's hardening in bichromate.

Oct. 5, 1892. Dr. Bumpus has proposed the formation of a Biological Club to be quite select and limited in number to ten, including the botany laboratory fellows. He is just the man to direct such a project, but he wants us to work it out ourselves.

Oct. 12, 1892. Today the Bumpuses are busy moving into their new house on Oriole Avenue. He should be very happy, for he has worked hard and made a place for himself in the scientific world.

Nov. 14, 1892. Dr. Bumpus has given Strauss and me the job of cataloguing the biological journals in the library. It will take quite a little time, but it will familiarize us with what is there, and that was probably in the back of Bumpus's head when he gave us the job.

"Bumpus's lifelong enjoyment of good humor and his fund of good stories are exemplified in the next entry.

Jan. 5, 1893. Last night he told a story about an old German who was repairing his bass viol. Would that I were able to reproduce the acting that he put into it and the expressions on his face as he told it. However, said the German in a fit of disgust, 'Ach! I haf now dot dat damn fiddle finished!' Then a dramatic pause, and *'Donner und Blitzen,* das glue pot it iss on der inside!'

April 24, 1893. Bumpus has one jolly custom with his class in invertebrates. They are now working on the lobster and of course use fresh material. After class we go down to the furnace room and roast the claws in the ashes. They are fine that way, with the Professor as toastmaster.

May 9, 1893. The Doctor invited Tower and me over to his new home on Oriole Avenue to dinner today, and we had a fine time. He had been out with his invertebrates class in the afternoon, collecting, and brought in a little striped snake in his glove. He has a weakness for snakes and can never pass one by. Carey, Jr., his young son, got right down on the carpet and played with the little snake to his heart's content, even crying when his bedtime came and he wasn't allowed to take it to bed with him."

Students who contemplated a medical career were given special and separate courses in biology—a plan that had the advantages of giving direction and purpose to undergraduate study, bringing students of similar ambitions together, and enabling them to meet and associate with practicing physicians and surgeons and thus to gain an understanding of the serious side of the profession. It also made clear to a certain few that a medical career was not for them. On the other hand, it gave valuable preparation to those who finally entered the medical school by familiarizing them with the purposes of medical instruction and biological research. Brown was possibly the first university to give an integrated premedical course.

Not satisfied with standardized osteology and illustrative charts, the students wanted bones with muscles on them. Accordingly, Professor Bumpus went to see President Andrews about the possibility of giving a class in human anatomy. He realized that the students could learn from the dissection of cats all that was necessary in their biological work, but he also appreciated what a stimulus human dissection would give the advanced students. With a characteristic smile the president said, "Professor, I don't want to know anything about it!"

With this backhanded encouragement Professor Bumpus obtained an unclaimed body from the medical examiner, and in an abandoned room under the roof a class in human anatomy was started.

One morning not long afterward Mrs. Bumpus was startled at the breakfast table by a look of consternation on her husband's face when he opened his morning paper. Without waiting to finish his coffee and without explanation he left the table and departed posthaste. In the front-page picture of a person reported missing he had recognized a strong resemblance to the cadaver his students were dissecting in the new course. Fortunately the parts of the body essential to proper interment had not been disfigured. Removing the body from Rhode Island Hall and returning it to the city morgue, where it could be "found" and identified, presented difficulties that it took Dr. Bumpus' genius for coping with the unusual to solve.

So active had the work of the biology department become, and so enthusiastic its members, that nothing which could minister to their ambitions was sacred. A story handed down from that period concerns an irate citizen of Providence who had missed his pet cat and felt certain that it had somehow reached the interior of Rhode Island Hall, where the biology laboratory was housed. He explained to the students carefully and with much agitation that if he whistled he was sure his cat would come running to him. One bright student, perhaps a bit callous from laboratory hours spent among dead animals, replied briefly, "Well, Mister, I'm sure you'll have to whistle long and loud for that cat."

A ponderous stuffed walrus, the memorial gift of some early class, was denounced as occupying space that might better be used for a laboratory table. Tradition had no restraining effect, and out went the walrus, along with a striding stuffed giraffe. Dissecting tables were moved into the sanctity of the museum. The cellar, from which the furnaces had been removed, became a miniature abbatoir, and what appeared to those on George Street as a newly constructed conservatory was in fact a congested animal house. One student, who later became a leading professor at Massachusetts Institute of Technology, after his first instruction in physiology installed apparatus for independent research in an abandoned coalbin. It was generally understood that at Brown marble slabs, mahogany trim, and nickel fittings were not a prerequisite for serious scientific work.

The Brown University catalogue of that time shows that courses of instruction were so arranged that a freshman who so desired could begin work in the biology laboratory in Rhode Island Hall the day he entered college and could continue to work every day for the next four years without breaking the continuity of his course. Even his vacations were not vacuums.

Bumpus' belief that help comes to those who help themselves was justified and enhanced by the gifts of Professor John Pierce, a man of pleasing personality and considerable means who lived near the university. In early life he had been connected with Harvard College. He was especially proficient in physics and chemistry. Professor Pierce enjoyed the companionship of the people at work in the laboratory and called upon them almost daily, intuitively noting their needs. The following day or soon after one would find unostentatiously left on the laboratory table a series of volumes or a valuable instrument appropriate to the problem at hand. He was the living equivalent of a handsome endowment, the liberal income of which was used with punctilious discretion.

In his history of the Brown biology department Professor Bumpus wrote: "The range of interest covered by the several workers in the department was almost absurdly broad. The proper teaching and distribution of material for 150 students, ranging from freshmen to seniors, were the obligations, but the graduate students were insatiable foci of absorption. The demand for dissecting materials was by no means temperate and sometimes required exhausting expeditions into the country along the shore, and even into the Bay. While one group was endeavoring to equip and operate a Bacteriological Laboratory, another group was consuming clay and mixing plaster in amateurish but commendable efforts at the production of anatomical models or geological relief maps. The wheels of microtomes were being rotated by those who had become interested in section cutting and slabs of wax were being destroyed in efforts to construct what were called 'enlarged reproductions.' Some were interested in making permanent anatomical preparations.

"Perhaps the outstanding event of the year was the biological survey of Narragansett Bay. In the winter it was suggested that if the students should vote to sacrifice their spring vacation and devote themselves to a study of the living fauna of the Bay, the time so spent would be a credit against the required biological courses during the balance of the year. The vote was overwhelmingly in the affirmative. A steam oyster dredge was engaged, a class of sixty students was divided into squads, skimming nets, spades, buckets and bottles were provided, and a vacation filled with experiences resulted. It was in late March and early April, but the season was backward. Sometimes the snow came in cold sheets and the water was like ice. The lee side of the Pilot House was far from comfortable, even with the 'heat control' of a wash boiler filled with steaming stew. All had a glorious time and fortunately there were no resulting cases of pneumonia. The whole thing resulted in bushels of specimens, gallons of alcoholics, and the storeroom was glutted with material that, it is presumed, has received no further attention.

"It was all biology in the broadest sense—unorthodox—but the students wanted it and it really assisted many in their ambition to live lives more satisfying and of great usefulness."

The press hailed this innovation in teaching as marking an epoch in the methods of study in American institutions throughout the country as well as at Brown University. "The results of this busy week of investigation," it was said, "with the various forms of life which have been discovered in the Bay, will soon be made public and will prove interesting not only to Rhode Islanders but to scientists everywhere."

Reviewing the fourth year of his administration, President Andrews stated: "I am impressed with the power of observatorial science, when taught in the best manner, to form the mind and stimulate a desire for learning. In no other spheres of the University life are these effects more discernible at present than in Zoology, Botany and Comparative Anatomy."

At this time, when Dr. Bumpus had the department of biology well organized and functioning to the satisfaction of President Andrews, he felt the need of broadening his knowledge and of meeting men in other parts of the world who were engaged in similar work. After making arrangements for the conduct of affairs in the department, Dr. Bumpus, with his wife and their small son, sailed for Europe in the fall of 1893. Both in England and on the Continent he visited leading educational and scientific institutions. He went to Plymouth and London, traveled up the Rhine as far as Wurzburg, visited Lucerne, and from there went to Genoa, Naples, Rome, and Milan, then to France and back to England. At Naples he remained long enough to be assigned a table temporarily at the famous marine laboratory of Dr. Anton Dohrn, and at Plymouth he was entertained at the well-known seaside station for fisheries, with whose officials he had been corresponding for some time.

This European peregrination was the first of a long series, for Bumpus was a prodigious traveler, whose natural inquisitiveness made him desirous of seeing as much as possible of the earth's surface.

Upon his return from Europe Dr. Bumpus conceived the idea of obtaining moral and financial support for his laboratory by inaugurating an informal organization of local physicians and interested friends, chiefly graduates of the university, to be known as the Biological Club. At that time biological laboratories were not regarded as essential adjuncts of hospitals, nor were they as common as they have since become. The instruments and methods in the department were therefore novel and interesting to many members of the club, who constituted a sort of visiting or advisory committee, which Dr. Bumpus believed, once they were informed and interested, would support his various projects. Such organizations of "friends" are now common, but at that time the idea was new.

The newly organized club met on certain evenings each month in Rhode Island Hall and invited lecturers on such subjects as methods of disinfection, antitoxin and diphtheria, tuberculosis, diseases of the skin, and diseases of the bones. It is probable that the present Arnold Laboratory, established through the splendid bequest of Dr. Oliver H. Arnold, was a result of friendships made at the Biological Club. Also, the collection of anatomical and other material which had accumulated in the rooms of the Rhode Island Medical Society and dated back to the time when Brown had a medical school and was truly a university, was turned over to the department of biology.

As a further result of the club Dr. Bumpus was appointed to the board of trustees of the Rhode Island Hospital and was made an honorary member of the Rhode Island Medical Society. At that time the Rhode Island Hospital did not have a laboratory of pathology, and it was through Dr. Bumpus' solicitation that the widow of Dr. Gustave Radeke, a philanthropic citizen of Providence, generously donated funds to establish one.

That the interest of the young professor reached afield into the community is attested by the appearance of his name not only on the board of trustees of the Rhode Island Hospital, from 1895 to 1901, but also on the board of management of the Rhode Island School of Design, from 1899 to 1901, and by his election to the presidency of the Audubon Society of Rhode Island. The organization of this society on October 20, 1897, was a culmination of the growing public protest against the unchecked slaughter of wild birds for commercial use. Ornithologists and nature lovers in general felt that a way must be found to save valuable species from extermination, particularly such waterfowl as gulls and terns, whose white wings were greatly sought after for the adornment of women's hats. One of Dr. Bumpus' first acts as president of the Rhode Island society was the launching of an educational campaign which resulted in protective legislation for birds and in discouraging the use of feathers for adornment.

Forty-four years later, on June 7, 1941, a group of Dr. Bumpus' old friends gathered together at the Kimball Bird Sanctuary of the Audubon Society of Rhode Island to honor him after his election as honorary president of the society he had helped to establish. A brochure, *Hermon Carey Bumpus, Naturalist*,[*] describes his role in the development and work of the society.

Dr. Bumpus' output of scientific papers was not large. His restless energy found more satisfaction in doing things than in sitting at a desk with a pen in his hand. Moreover, he was always more interested in making it possible for others to record the results of their studies than in writing scientific papers himself. Nevertheless, particularly during the Woods Hole years, he did produce several contributions to the biological problems and techniques of the day.

Bumpus was much concerned, for example, with examining the basis of Darwin's theory of natural selection, which was then front-page news in the biological world. In the decades immediately after the publication in 1859 of *The Origin of Species* biologists were chiefly engaged in theoretical discus-

[*] Prepared by Alice Hall Walter. Providence, Rhode Island: Audubon Society of Rhode Island, 1943. 46 pp.

sion and argument over the fertile ideas Darwin presented in this book. Bumpus was one of the first to turn away from the endless talk and seek refuge in experimentation to determine the validity or lack of it in Darwin's theory. He realized that analysis of variation lay at the very root of the problems biologists were discussing, and he proceeded directly to ways and means of developing quantitative techniques for measuring variability.

In the early nineties biometry, the application of statistics to biological data, was a new technique, and Bumpus was one of the pioneers in its development. A period followed in which nearly every investigator working at Woods Hole pursued the biometrical method, and all that appeared necessary in carrying through a piece of research was to secure a mass of data from which, with the magic of mathematics, a biological rabbit could be coaxed out of the magician's hat.

The eggs of the English sparrow were the material for the first of Bumpus' papers on variation.* These common birds had only recently been introduced into America and had rapidly overrun their new environment. It was thought that the eggs of these immigrants exhibited increased variability in form, size, and color. By subjecting to biometric techniques two lots of 868 eggs each, one lot from England and the other from the United States, Bumpus established the fact that the eggs of the imported birds showed greater variability. This enhanced variability he attributed to the fact that all sorts of individual deviations had a chance to survive in the new environment, where the forces of natural selection no longer operated, as they had in England, to produce eggs conforming to a standard successful in that environment.

Whatever the ultimate validity of his conclusions, the paper represented a valiant attempt to experiment with data of variation and natural selection, rather than merely to

* *The Variations and Mutations of the Introduced Sparrow, Passer Domesticus.* Lecture at the Marine Biological Laboratory, 1897.

speculate about the matter—certainly a step in the right direction.

In a similar piece of biometric work Bumpus employed a small tidal zone snail, the periwinkle, *Litorina littorea*, which had appeared from European shores within the memory of living men and had spread in great abundance all along the Atlantic Coast.* Bumpus wanted to determine whether these molluscan immigrants showed greater variability in their new environment than in the region from which they came. Obviously such a comparison could be made only by statistical methods. So lots of a thousand shells each were collected from ten stations along the Atlantic shore extending from the mouth of the St. Croix River in New Brunswick to Long Island Sound. These were all painstakingly measured, and their standard deviations and coefficients of variability were computed. When the results were compared with data obtained from comparable lots of British shells, it was found that the shells from every Atlantic station registered greater variability than the European shells.

In another contribution appearing at about the same time, Bumpus' approach and attitude of mind are indicated in the opening paragraph. "We are so in the habit of referring carelessly to the process of natural selection, and of invoking its aid whenever some pet theory seems a little feeble," he wrote, "that we forget we are really using a hypothesis that still remains unproved, and that specific examples of the destruction of animals of known physical disability are very infrequent. Even if the theory of natural selection were as firmly established as Newton's theory of the attraction of gravity, scientific method would still require frequent examination of its claims, and scientific honesty should welcome such examination and insist on its thoroughness."†

This investigation was inspired by an experience in

* "The Variations and Mutations of the Introduced *Litorina*," *Zool. Bull.*, vol. 1, no. 5, 1898.

† *The Elimination of the Unfit, as Illustrated by the Introduced Sparrow, Passer Domesticus.* Marine Biological Laboratory, 1898.

HERMON CAREY BUMPUS

February 1898. Dr. Bumpus was coming up College Hill one day after an uncommonly severe storm of snow, rain, and sleet when he noticed, scattered about the ground dead or exhausted, a large number of English sparrows from the colony wintering in the vines of the old athenaeum. He was quick to see that here before his eyes was an experiment in nature, all ready for analysis. He collected as many of the sparrows as he could and bore them away to the laboratory. Of the 136 birds he collected, 72 revived and 64 perished. His analysis showed that "the birds which perished, perished not through accident, but because they were physically disqualified, and that the birds which survived, survived because they possessed certain physical characteristics that enabled them to withstand the intensity of this particular phase of selective elimination and distinguished them from their more unfortunate companions."*

Biometric methods were again followed in analyzing the data. Variation in the two groups of sparrows was determined by carefully measuring each individual for ten different factors, such as length, alar extent, and weight, and combining the results. It turned out that the process of selective elimination was in each instance more severe with the extremely variable individuals, in whatever direction the extreme occurred. He concluded, "It is quite as dangerous to be conspicuously above a certain standard of organic excellence as it is to be below the standard. It is the *type* that nature favors, and this type is brought about by natural selection and its elimination of the unfit."

* See also an article by J. A. Harris entitled "Neglected Paper on Natural Selection in the English Sparrow; Professor Bumpus on Elimination of the Unfit," in *American Naturalist*, 45: 314–18 (May 1911). In a paper read before the Providence Art Club on January 5, 1945, Professor J. Walter Wilson, Chairman, Department of Biology, Brown University, states: "One of Dr. Bumpus's investigations on evolution in which the English sparrow, the Providence Athenaeum, and a New England blizzard all played parts is cited as a 'classical work' in the most up-to-date book on evolution, i.e., *Evolution—the Modern Synthesis*, by Julian Huxley. I will not here discuss any of his other researches, but will merely say this: that any man whose works were all in the field of science would be content if one work were to be cited half a century after its publication as a classic."

A final study in this quartet of inquiries into the workings of biological variation involved a recent invention and its application to biometric analysis.* Variation was known to occur in the number of vertebrae forming the backbone of the mud puppy *Necturus*, and in the position on the vertebral column where the pelvic girdle is attached. The accumulation of data on such problems was painfully slow, for it involved laborious and time-consuming dissection. While Dr. Bumpus was working on this problem, Roentgen's discovery of the X-ray was reported. At once he saw the possibility of using the X-ray instead of dissection to test variations in skeletal structure. A Crookes tube was obtained, and during the entire summer of 1896 Professor Bumpus worked with the X-ray, photographing a hundred specimens of *Necturus* from a jarful of "alcoholics" that had escaped previous dissection. In a minimum of time, and without the necessity of tedious dissection or in any way mutilating his mud puppies, he had photographic records of the variation in the number of vertebrae and the position of the pelvic girdle. So far as is known, this was the first use of the X-ray in the study of skeletons.

Dr. Bumpus gave numerous lectures on and demonstrations of the new X-ray to nearby scientific societies and colleges. The dangers of the new rays were not then appreciated, and his escape from the severe burns to which other pioneers in this field succumbed seems little short of miraculous. He took his X-ray machine to the Rhode Island Hospital and located with it a needle in a patient's foot. Dr. Walter Munro then successfully removed the needle. This was the first time X-rays were used in connection with surgery in Rhode Island, and one of the first operations ever performed with the assistance of X-rays.

In these four studies by biometric methods Professor Bumpus showed unusual insight and imagination in mark-

* "A Contribution to the Study of Variation," *Jour. Morphology*, vol. 12. February 1897.

ing out his problems, and clever invention and initiative in devising means for their solution.

It was natural that women students, of whom there were 149 registered in the women's college of Brown University, should desire certain special courses in the popular biology department. To give them such instruction Miss Ada Wing, a graduate of Wellesley and also of Brown, where she had received the master's degree, was appointed instructor in physiology, hygiene, and sanitary science. Not only did she perform her duties efficiently, but she also extended the general interest of the women students in biology to such an extent that they contributed fifty dollars to the maintenance of the "Women's Table" at the famous marine biological station at Naples.

Other advances were made in the department. Forty compound microscopes were added to the equipment—an outstanding acquisition. The accumulated scientific papers of the department were combined in the first volume of a series entitled Contributions from the Biological Laboratory of Brown University. A very creditable library of biological books and periodicals had been assembled, keeping the department conversant with biological activities throughout the world. Along with the department staff and the graduate students, this collection was taken each summer to Woods Hole and for several years constituted virtually the entire library of the Marine Biological Laboratory.

Of a total attendance of 866 at Brown University in 1897, 354 were studying in the department of biology. Five hundred and twenty-three students, including those studying with Professor Packard, had work in Rhode Island Hall. The inadequacy of the building to accommodate the growing number of students was even more obvious in September 1898. The class in anatomy numbered sixty and was too large for any available room in Rhode Island Hall. To provide space for the class the museum was reluctantly cleared. Most of the cases were removed, specimens were stored away, more tables were improvised, instructors were pressed into service, and the work went on. North Hall, for many years a cherished lecture room, was partially dismantled and transformed into another laboratory. From the beginning the policy had been to rely upon objective instruction and reduce talking to a minimum, to let students see, touch, and even smell, rather than passively listen to someone lecture on how nature behaved.

Fully appreciating that the rapid growth of his department demanded greater financial support than was assignable in the university budget to any one department, Professor Bumpus looked about for other ways of getting the needed funds. The favorable publicity that had attended his earlier collecting trip down Narragansett Bay convinced him that some arrangement of mutual benefit to the biology department of the university and the state fisheries could be worked out. He explained to Governor Lippitt his desire to extend into the bay the practical work of his department, in so far as it had to do with marine life of economic value. The governor had the power of appointment to both the State Commission on Inland Fisheries and the State Shellfish Commission. Knowing that positions on the latter carried salaries and so were considered political spoils, Professor Bumpus asked to be appointed to the State Commission on Inland Fisheries, in which membership was purely honorary and was usually held by sportsmen. To the governor it seemed a bit farfetched that a man who wanted to work in Narragansett Bay should seek an appointment on the Inland Fisheries Commission. However, the professor had a persuasive way and since there was no salary attached to the position he asked for, the governor granted his request.

After receiving his appointment Professor Bumpus at once purchased the appurtenances of a sportsman, including hip boots, rod, reel, and a bottle. He so endeared himself to the old sportsmen of the commission that, after several convivial fishing trips together, they agreed that a lobster, starfish, or crab was an inland fish as far as the law was concerned, if the learned doctor said so. As a result they backed him in his requests to the legislature for funds for his students who were studying the habits of these creatures. In this way the bay and biology were brought together, to the benefit of both. But the union produced some interesting editorials on the subject of whether a lobster was a fish in the eyes of the law or whether it should be regarded as game.

In reviewing this period Dr. Bumpus wrote: "A large old abandoned scow had for several years been lying half buried in the mud midway between Red and Washington bridges. In the spring of 1899, although it was doubtless unfair to the graduate students and certainly unauthorized by the administration to add ship carpentry and navigation to the already ultracomprehensive courses in biology, impressment took place. After rather long and uncleanly labor of the combined membership of the department—women excluded—a towboat was engaged and 'the ambition of the laboratory' floated down the bay into Wickford Harbor, where the houseboat was anchored, just in time to avoid its perpetual submergence. The contraption proved to be a temporary godsend, and in addition to its primary function it provided a moderate income for a few impecunious students. Its operation by the department resulted in research conducted by A. D. Mead which so enhanced the value of the important lobster industry that they were recognized at the 4th International Fisheries Congress by a medal awarded to Dr. Mead, with assurances that the results of his labors constituted the essential economic event of the year."

Bumpus was fast becoming known as a man of ideas with the energy necessary to carry them into effect. Much earlier, in February 1890, he had been elected to membership in the Boston Society of Natural History, and in the following year to Phi Beta Kappa. In May 1900 he was chosen for membership in the honorary scientific fraternity, Sigma Xi. He had been chairman of the National Committee for Bird Protection, the other two members being Frank M. Chapman and Ralph Hoffman, both leading ornithologists. With these able assistants he mapped out a six-point program that became the basis for the organization of the National Association of Audubon Societies of America. Upon the incorporation of the association Dr. Bumpus was chosen a director. He had already served as vice-president of the American Society of Naturalists and also of the American Morphological Society. So it is not surprising that when Morris K. Jesup, New York capitalist and philanthropist, sought someone to assist him in his honorary position as president of the American Museum of Natural History, his choice fell upon Professor Bumpus.

Throughout his long life, both in small matters and in great, it was characteristic of Professor Bumpus that he acted as a catalyzer. When the resulting development or organization was progressing smoothly, he gradually retired from the scene, though never before he had made his complete contribution.

At Brown University his fundamental purpose was to effect a molecular union of the traditional undergraduate teaching with the new ideals of scholarship and research he had found at Clark University. Within a decade he had accomplished this purpose with eminent success. He felt free therefore to accept the opportunity that a great institution like the American Museum of Natural History offered him.

CHAPTER V

The American Museum of Natural History, 1900-1910

WORKING conditions at the American Museum of Natural History contrasted sharply with those Dr. Bumpus had experienced at Woods Hole and Providence, where the question of adequate funds was always paramount. In his new position this problem was most expeditiously taken care of by the board of trustees, composed of the leading financiers of New York.

A reciprocal agreement, stimulating both to public expenditure and to private munificence, had been inaugurated at the time the Metropolitan Museum of Art and the American Museum of Natural History were founded. The City of New York, assisted from time to time by state aid, erected and maintained the buildings and also appropriated funds for the payment of salaries, but funds for purchasing collections and financing exploring expeditions were donated by private citizens and the boards of trustees. Since the appropriations for salaries were seldom sufficient, the difference was made up by income from the endowment fund.

In the days before the federal income tax it was the custom of the president of the board of trustees of the American Museum to report the budgetary needs for the next year to the finance committee. It usually happened that J. P. Morgan, who was generally chairman of this committee, would head the subscription list with a donation of from ten to twenty thousand dollars and would then pass this paper around the table. Other members followed by pledging lesser amounts, but they were always sufficiently liberal to avoid the disfavor of Mr. Morgan, who was a mighty force in the financial world. In this way hundreds of thousands of dollars for scientific expeditions and the preparation of specimens were raised in a matter of a few minutes.

The president of the museum's board since 1881 had been Morris Ketchum Jesup, who had amassed a fortune in the development of western railroads and from the increase in value of his large holdings of New York real estate. An extraordinary man with little formal schooling, he used his great wealth to give others the educational advantages he had been denied.

A paragraph from his annual report of 1884 illustrates his breadth of vision and his idealistic nature: "To the multitude shut up in stone walls, to whom are denied an acquaintance with the beauty of natural objects or the study of nature in its usual aspects and conditions, the advantage of your museum is that it affords opportunity; and out of a great number who look on vaguely and experience only the healthful excitement of a natural curiosity, one here and there may be found endowed with special aptitude and tastes. Perhaps some child of genius whose susceptibilities and faculties once aroused and quickened will repay in the field of discovery and science through the force of some new law in its manifold applications all your expenditure a hundred fold."

Jesup took great pride in the museum and usually lunched there once or twice a week. At a time when sideburns were to the philanthropist what the helmet and billy were to the corner policeman, the austere Jesup wore full sideburns that fairly radiated dignity. Once as he was entering the Metropolitan Museum of Art, a guard stopped him and told him he would have to check his cane. He paused a moment, then with much dignity took a calling card from his wallet and said, "Take this to your director and inform him that Morris K. Jesup always carries his cane."

During his presidency Jesup contributed a million dollars to a museum that had had an annual income of only fifteen thousand dollars when he assumed his duties, and by his will he left it a million more. Significant of his great interest in the welfare of the museum is a paragraph in his will:

"I have been its president since 1881. Since that time I have directed a great part of my life, my time, my thoughts and my attention to its interests. I believe it to be today one of the most effective agencies which exist in the City of New York for furnishing education, innocent amusement and instruction to the public."

When Dr. Bumpus came to the museum in 1900, as assistant to Mr. Jesup and curator of invertebrate zoology, it was already a great institution with an amazing wealth of material and equipment, both actual and potential. The exhibits, however, were not of very high standards. Throughout the nineteenth century natural history museums had been looked upon as depositories for collections of specimens, many of them badly prepared. The museum had case after case of stuffed birds, all perched on the same type of pedestal, with scientific name attached, but giving the visitor no useful or interesting information and frequently no indication of origin. Even the scientist knew nothing about many specimens put on exhibition. For example, a shellfish that looked very much like a clam might be labeled merely "*Tellina rugosa* from the Island of Opara"—information that only completed the bewilderment of the ordinary visitor. The fact was that only those who collected the specimens gained much knowledge from them.

Dr. Bumpus thought of the museum not primarily as a storehouse for natural history specimens serving as research material for the scientific staff, but as an educational institution with a role different from that of school or college. He believed therefore that the more attractive were the exhibits the greater would be the public interest, and hence the greater their value.

In an article for a popular magazine of the day Bumpus wrote: "Dreary series of stuffed animals are giving place to realistic groups in an outdoors atmosphere. The pedantry of scientific labels is being silenced. Molds of exquisite workmanship have succeeded noisome alcoholics, and exhibition halls have become airy, cleanly, and architecturally attractive." Of the "noisome alcoholics" he wrote: "Many still remember the exhibition of what were euphemistically called 'spirit specimens.' This marked the glass jar epoch of museum development. Few museum officers had the courage to open these receptacles and few visitors derived benefit from inspecting distorted images of disintegrating tissue."

James L. Clark, who eventually became head of the museum's department of preparation and installation, explains how Dr. Bumpus went about carrying out his new ideas.

"Dr. Bumpus was responsible for bringing me to the museum. It was in 1902, when I was at the Rhode Island School of Design, that word came through from the director of the American Museum that he was looking for a young sculptor, and I happened to be picked from the modeling class as one who might possibly fill the bill. I came to New York and called on Dr. Bumpus personally, and of course was very much impressed by the institution and by him. It was all rather awe-inspiring for a young fellow from a small town. But what impressed me most and what I have always remembered was his kindness and sympathy. He gave me a great deal of time and took me through the halls and pointed out the bad work in taxidermy that had been done. He explained how he wanted it improved by showing me some of Charles H. Knight's exquisite drawings and models of animals, some modern but mostly prehistoric, and all crammed full of action and realism.

"At that time Carl Akeley had developed his new method of sculpturing animals at the Field Museum, but he was keeping it a secret. In his progressive way Dr. Bumpus realized the importance of this development and immediately wanted the American Museum to have the advantage of this advanced technique. Since Akeley would not give it out Dr. Bumpus had to approach the problem in some other way. His first step was to look for a young sculptor with art training and let him get technical training in taxidermy from some of the older and more staid taxidermists at the museum. This was a constructive way of going at it, and a policy I have followed ever since in building up the preparation department. It is certainly far easier to teach an artist simple mechanics than it is to teach a mechanic art.

"It was not long after that Dr. Bumpus brought Akeley up to the preparation department and introduced me to him. Shortly afterward Akeley told Dr. Bumpus that if he would send me out to Chicago he, Akeley, would give me all his secrets. This came about—through Dr. Bumpus's way of going after things instead of waiting for them to come to him—much to the benefit of the museum.

"For the next six years I was in the museum, until I resigned and went to Africa. During these six years I saw a great deal of Dr. Bumpus, and my first opinion of him never changed. He was aggressive, astute, and very progressive, but always kind and sympathetic, though I know from what I heard occasionally that he could carry on a good fight if the situation demanded it.

"One of the finest halls we have today is the Northwest Coast Indians Hall, which Dr. Bumpus conceived and rebuilt with the help of Mr. Taylor. Today it stands comparison very well with halls built more recently. It was based on so sound a conception that in my opinion it has in no way become obsolete. It shows remarkably good taste. I think this was one of Dr. Bumpus's strong points—that he exercised not only good judgment but also good taste."

Dr. Bumpus had the faculty of robbing science of its mystery and formidability and of presenting it in so interesting and vivid a manner that it became popular as well as

Hermon Carey Bumpus (from the painting by Howard E. Smith in Sayles Hall, Brown University)

ABOVE, *American Museum of Natural History.* BELOW, *A bungalow from the Philippine exhibit at the St. Louis Exposition became the Bumpus summer home*

easily understood. He was fertile in suggestions and constantly saw new ways of making exhibits interesting. For instance, instead of labeling a 15- or 20-foot slice of the giant sequoia "*Sequoia gigantea*, found in California," he placed a series of cards radiating from the center, each recording some great event occurring in the world's history at the time the particular ring thus marked was growing.

At the end of Dr. Bumpus' first year at the museum President Jesup sent him the following letter:

DEAR PROF. BUMPUS:—

I will not allow the year to close without my expressing to you the gratitude I feel to you for the work you have performed for the Museum and myself since you came into relations with us. . . . Your help, courage, fidelity, and ability have helped me so much and been so grateful to me that I want to say so to you and to thank you for all you have done. The light seems to be clearing, the clouds are rolling away, and the new year comes in circumstances better and brighter than I expected. I have learned to place confidence in you and to rely on your judgment and ability. I trust your connection with the Museum for 1902 will be more pleasant and agreeable than the past year. After tomorrow I propose to take up with you the question of changing the position you now hold to one that would imply more dignity and honor to yourself.

Wishing you a happy and successful new year, I am

Sincerely yours,

MORRIS K. JESUP

In fulfillment of the promise in this letter, Dr. Bumpus was made the first director of the American Museum of Natural History, with expanding responsibilities and duties.

Someone has remarked that when Bumpus went to New York, museums of nearly every type were just thawing out of their ice age. This thawing process was considerably accelerated, both at the American Museum and throughout the country, by his successful efforts to develop the educational functions of museums. The increasing confidence placed in him by President Jesup proved a great stimulus to his ability, and under his direction the museum, in research, exhibition, and education, soon took its place among the leading institutions in its field.

As director Dr. Bumpus was in charge of the administrative as well as the scientific work of the museum. On the administrative side he was responsible not only for the routine running of the institution but also for all matters connected with its material growth. It was his duty to recommend alterations and new construction and to supervise both while they were in progress. He was responsible also for the annual budget and for detailed data concerning the disbursement of all public moneys.

On the scientific side he had jurisdiction over all exploring expeditions, scientific publications, the installation of exhibits, and the maintenance of an adequate scientific staff. He was also responsible for various forms of museum extension, such as special exhibits in connection with international affairs. Another duty was that of appearing before governmental groups in support of legislative measures involving appropriations by city and state.

Not long after assuming his new duties Dr. Bumpus issued a special invitation to the children of the New York schools to visit the museum for a nature talk to be given on a certain day. As the hour approached he sensed that something unusual was happening in the street, and looking from the window he saw that the approaches to the museum were blocked with thousands of children. Realizing that only a fraction of the throng could be taken care of in the lecture room, he hastily marshaled the entire museum force to handle the emergency. As the children entered, they were allocated to various exhibition halls of the vast building, and there were entertained by the curators and the scientific staff, summarily pressed into service. The talks were no less instructive because impromptu.

The interest of the school children, so dramatically demonstrated, was turned to advantage. As soon as possible, provision was made for periodic visits to the museum, a special department of education was set up under the direction of George H. Sherwood, a former graduate student at Brown University and Woods Hole, and the large collections of lantern slides owned by the museum were put to use in illustrated lectures upon subjects the children were studying in school. Traveling collections of natural history specimens were prepared and were sent around to the different public schools by truck. The museum was being humanized by making its vast resources available and intelligible to the people, and especially to the school children.

A member of Dr. Bumpus' staff reports: "In the conduct of the various departments of the museum the new director was a natural leader. His active imagination and dynamic energy put him a pace ahead of his fellow scientists, and his enthusiasm and fairness always brought him the loyalty of his staff."

Robert Cushman Murphy, later a curator but at that time a junior member of the scientific staff, writes:

"Museum exhibits depend very largely upon one kind or another of manual and mechanical techniques, and here Dr. Bumpus had a great initial advantage because of his own artistic and constructional ability, his personal handiness with tools, and his power of working out in his imagination all the little tricks of showmanship that might go into the finished product. He never forgot that the *feeling* of an exhibit and the need for it to tell a story were quite as important as its factual truthfulness. He was probably one of the first museum men to demand frankly that every exhibit should be entertaining.

"Another point about Bumpus was that he could lay an idea before one of his associates with enthusiasm and fervor, transfer some of the flame that was in himself, and thereafter let the man and the job alone until he was sent for to come back and see its progress. He never hounded anybody in whom he had reason to feel confidence. He was always overjoyed, in fact, if the leaven he had set working produced a result somewhat different from the one he had envisioned, provided the story was told as well or better. This gave him the advantage that is a characteristic of all truly competent administrators. He knew how to delegate authority and responsibility, which gave him opportunity to forget one problem after another, at least for the time, and to turn his ambition to the new ones that were always bubbling up in his brain.

"Dr. Bumpus kept in closer personal touch with everybody on his staff, and indeed with all the employees of his institution, than any other museum director of whom I have ever heard. I am in a good position to know this, because in 1906 and 1907 I occupied one of the humblest posts in the American Museum, and yet I doubt whether a week passed throughout the course of the year in which Dr. Bumpus did not come briskly into whatever room I was occupying, exchange a greeting, ask a few questions, and then scoot along to the next fellow. I believe that he had literally everybody known by name, had a clear idea of what the individual was about, and within a short time had made a personal estimate that was rarely far from correct.

"He seldom took part in long discussions with anybody on the job, and he often devoted not more than five or ten minutes to conferences that many persons would have spread over an hour or longer. He was so quick and direct that I suspect the necessity of being tactful went more or less against his grain. This may be one of the reasons why he never had any difficulty with his peers and subordinates, whereas at times certain members of the board to which he was responsible would have their dignity offended."

Dr. Frank M. Chapman, an active curator of the museum from 1888 until his retirement half a century later, collaborated heartily with Dr. Bumpus in carrying out his plans, particularly in the conception and execution of the elaborate bird groups that have made the museum famous.

He dedicated his book *Camps and Cruises of an Ornithologist* to Dr. Bumpus, and in his *Autobiography of a Bird Lover* he writes, in explaining the development of the idea of exhibiting birds in groups in settings simulating their natural surroundings:

"The Cobb Island group, like that of Bird Rock, stands today as it was made, and marks a further step in the development of the habitat group idea. The background is curved, its top and sides concealed, the light comes wholly from above, and the illusion of reality is thereby greatly increased. One seems to be looking through a window on nature itself. This type of case was devised by Dr. Hermon C. Bumpus, then Director of the Museum, and my enthusiastic cooperator in the introduction of new methods of exhibition."

One of the many functions of the American Museum was to sponsor expeditions for the collection of materials and for exploration. In 1910 Dr. Bumpus himself went to Mexico and Yucatán to investigate the Mayan ruins of Chichen Itzá and the Aztec remains at Mitla.

All these enterprises and projects naturally brought Dr. Bumpus into official and often intimate contact with many important and interesting people. His diaries make mention of Walter Page, Earl Grey, Andrew Carnegie, President Charles W. Eliot of Harvard, Helen Gould, Edward Everett Hale, Gifford Pinchot, Samuel Gompers, D. O. Mills, John D. Rockefeller, Jr., Robert De Forest, Sir Caspar Purdon Clarke, Angelo Heilprin, Robert E. Peary, and Captain Bonsall, who accompanied Elisha Kent Kane in his search for Sir John Franklin.

In an exciting article in the *Saturday Evening Post* of September 14, 1929, Roy Chapman Andrews tells the story of how he as a young man was sent by Director Bumpus to recover a whale's skeleton and later helped in the construction of the first and only life-sized model of earth's largest mammal. It was striking evidence that the exhibition of material collected through field expeditions was to be undertaken in a big way by the new director. Later Andrews made a series of expeditions to the Gobi Desert for the museum, in search of traces of early man. On one of these expeditions he made his famous discovery of fossil dinosaur eggs.

In a book entitled *Under a Lucky Star, A Lifetime of Adventure*,* Andrews tells how, as a boy naturalist from the Middle West, he came to seek a position in the museum. He says of its director: "I will never forget my first impression of Dr. Bumpus in 1906 when I came to the American Museum looking for a job. It was of great vitality and tremendous energy being held in check with difficulty. He seemed like a race horse at the post ready to leap down the track at the starter's flag. He brought with him something fresh and vital whenever he entered a room." Bumpus, with his instinctive ability to appraise capacity and promise, gave the young man an opportunity to prove his worth, and Andrews in time became the director of the museum.

Through President Jesup the American Museum was closely associated with the Peary Arctic Club, which financed the numerous attempts and final success of Robert E. Peary to reach the North Pole. In 1895, in response to an appeal from Mrs. Peary, Mr. Jesup had fitted out a relief expedition to bring Peary home from the Arctic. This was the beginning of his interest in the work of the explorer, which he continued in successive contributions to Peary's expeditions. Jesup was rewarded when Peary's efforts culminated in the discovery of the North Pole in 1909 and when his collections were deposited in the American Museum. From one of the expeditions Peary brought back a 30-ton meteorite, the largest then known. It was brought to the museum on a dray drawn by a team of twenty-four horses and placed before the entrance.

Not long afterward two Colorado cowboys reported finding another meteorite of about equal size, and the director im-

* New York: Viking Press, 1943.

mediately sent out representatives of the museum to acquire it. By the time they arrived in Colorado a rather interesting lawsuit was in progress. The cowboys claimed that meteorites, wandering in the fields of heaven, were similar to unbranded cattle and that like cattle they became the property of those who discovered them and put on their brand, as the men had done with their find. The owner of the land where the fallen meteorite was discovered claimed that it was a mineral, which it certainly was, and said that the laws of mineral rights should therefore prevail. Unfortunately for the legal status of meteorites, the case was settled out of court, with the assistance of the museum representatives, and the meteorite was shipped to New York.

It was placed in the museum foyer, near the one Peary had brought back from the North. With the numerous smaller examples of celestial wonders surrounding them, they constituted the finest collection of meteorites in the world. An attendant in this hall reported hearing a clergyman remark that he had always preached that God was good, but that after viewing these visitors from the heavens he would in the future add that he felt the Creator was also a bit careless, for if one had ever struck a church it would certainly have demolished it.

An impressive way of demonstrating the solar system was installed in the Hall of Meteorites at Dr. Bumpus' suggestion. A six-inch lighted globe was placed in the center to represent the sun, and other lights of proper size, representing the planets, were placed at appropriate distances, so that one could gain an accurate impression of the distance and size of the planets as seen from the sun and of the size of the sun as seen from any of the planets.

At this time Dr. Bumpus performed an act of kindness in helping Matt Hensen, a Negro, who had been Peary's only companion on his last, forced march to the Pole. As so often happens, the work of the colored man had been forgotten in the glory and public acclaim of the discovery. Dr. Bumpus gave Hensen a set of lantern slides of the Arctic regions, and with them he was able to rehabilitate himself by giving popular lectures among his people.

Up to this time Arctic exploration had been considered extremely hazardous, and those who took part in it were always greeted as heroes upon their return. Vilhjalmur Stefansson, who thought otherwise, presented to Director Bumpus his then novel idea that a white man could live off the country as well as an Eskimo. He received a sympathetic response, and Bumpus later wrote in all modesty, "I had a hand in getting him into the North." In his two books, *Friendly Arctic* and *Life with the Eskimos*, Stefansson upsets many earlier views, both lay and scientific, concerning the rigors of the Arctic. He gratefully acknowledges in all his books the help and encouragement given him by Dr. Bumpus, and as a more concrete token of esteem he named one of the mountains he discovered after Bumpus.

In 1903, after the discovery of radium by the Curies in 1902, Dr. Bumpus obtained some of the precious uranium mineral for exhibit in the museum. For the next few days the attendance broke all records, and the police were required to handle the crowds.

At the close of the St. Louis Exposition Dr. Bumpus was successful in obtaining for the museum the valuable Philippine exhibit which had been one of the main attractions of the fair. In the meantime, under the direction of Ralph W. Tower, one of Bumpus' early graduate students at Brown, the museum library had been transformed from a miscellaneous collection of odds and ends into one of the most comprehensive scientific libraries in the world. At Bumpus' suggestion the stilted Latin of the library bookplate had been altered to read: *For the people, For education, For science.*

Bumpus' work at the museum had not gone unnoticed by other educational institutions. In 1905 the honorary degree of Doctor of Science was conferred upon him by his alma mater, and President W. H. P. Faunce pronounced this appropriate citation: "Hermon Carey Bumpus of the class of 1884, notable student of physical life, inspiring teacher, approved administrator, founder of the Biological Department of Brown University, accomplishing with slender means enduring results, Director of the American Museum of Natural History." Tufts conferred an honorary Doctor of Science degree in the same year, and in 1909 Clark University conferred upon him, her oldest alumnus, the distinction of a Doctor of Laws degree.

In 1904, with the work at the museum well in hand, Dr. Bumpus once more took his family to Europe. There he visited the museums of England and the Continent and not only familiarized himself with the methods of administration and installation but also became personally acquainted with men prominent in museum work.

On this trip Dr. Bumpus met in England an elderly retired English officer who early in life had been stationed in New Zealand, where he had collected some forty-odd tattooed heads of the aborigines. The native tattooing was so beautiful and so appreciated by these people that when a member of the family died his head, properly tanned, was preserved. In this way the natives were able to keep in personal contact, as it were, with their ancestors.

With the advent of the white man these heads came to have a commercial value, ever increasing as they became more scarce. A sea captain, upon inquiring if there were any to be had, was told, "Not now, but if you will look over the live ones and tell us which one you would like, we'll have it tanned and ready for you on your next voyage!" England naturally had to put a stop to this incentive to homicide among her subjects and forbade the exportation of tanned human heads under penalty of fine and imprisonment. As a result there were very few specimens in even the largest museums, and the retired colonel's collection represented more than were to be found in all the museums together.

Dr. Bumpus was therefore delighted to acquire the collection for the American Museum of Natural History, and brought the heads home in his private luggage. When the customs officer opened the trunks in New York and saw forty human faces looking at him he was, to say the least, taken aback. He proclaimed that during his many years as an inspector this was the most unusual consignment of goods he had ever seen. Sorely at a loss to know how to classify them for the customs duties, he ended by listing them as "leather goods."

Dr. Bumpus was instrumental in forming the American Association of Museums and on May 15, 1906, became the first president of the association. In the July 1906 issue of *World's Work*, a popular magazine of the day, a full-page picture of Dr. Bumpus appeared with the caption "First President of the new Association of Museums, whose work in the Museum of Natural History in New York is revolutionizing museum methods." Nor was his work without international recognition, for in 1910 King Carol I of Roumania transmitted to him through the American minister at Bucharest the Patent and Insignia of the Commander's Cross of the Order of the Crown of Roumania. The importance of Bumpus' influence upon the educational and scientific work of the American museum was becoming known both in the United States and abroad.

Regarding the museum's work Dr. Bumpus wrote: "The activities of an institution of this kind take expression in two different directions—scientific investigation and education. The latter is absolutely dependent upon the former, and no institution of the character of the American Museum of Natural History can adequately present the various lines of scientific discovery without maintaining a number of field expeditions and encouraging research at home in the laboratories of the institution. The results of this exploration and investigation may be made known through scientific publications, lectures and demonstrations in exhibition halls. The absolute necessity of scientific work as a foundation for the educational work is taken for granted.

"A museum's obligation to the public, however, must cover not only the range of activity of the members of the scientific staff, but the entire range of human knowledge so far as the various branches of natural history are concerned.

"For example, the collections illustrating the subject of mineralogy should be so installed as to give the visitor a full knowledge of the physical and chemical characteristics of minerals as well as the uses of minerals in the arts, etc., even though the museum may not be equipped with laboratories or supplied with men of science that one would find in a technical school making a specialty of metallurgy. It would be a sadly incomplete museum that put on exhibition only material that had been collected by members of the staff and of interest only to members of the scientific staff. The collections ought to illustrate the subject instead of a man's work. It is of no interest to the public that this collection of shells from the shores of the Atlantic was made by some particular man. The exhibits in an institution of this nature should be made primarily for presenting in an ample manner various scientific subjects and not for the mere exhibition of specimens. The exhaustive collection of specimens belongs more to the workroom, where they should be available to visiting scientists. The so-called exhibition halls should be jealously preserved for imparting of information and the specimens carefully selected. The novel feature of sending artists into the field to get atmosphere for the installation of the animal groups illustrates how important their proper exhibition has become."

In the museum field, as in his university work, Dr. Bumpus held that both research and teaching were necessary for discharging the obligation of the institution as a whole to those in whose interest it was founded and maintained. Although he had been appointed to the Faculty of Pure

Science at Columbia University in 1905 and his name was among those starred in the then current edition of *Men of Science*, he believed that the first obligations of a public natural history museum were to the public. He felt that the necessity of scientific work as a foundation for the educational program would be taken for granted, for he wrote: "The man who never learns is a dead teacher. The museum that is not actively and ambitiously contributing to science is a poor institution."

He believed too that collections were more important than collectors and that the exhibited collections should illustrate the subject rather than the erudition of the curators. "There was a time," he said, "when curators felt that an intelligible label was an administrative blunder, and that a visitor should be made humble through conviction of personal ignorance. The idea that a museum exists in order that certain collections may be exhibited has been found fallacious. It assumed that the specimen was of more value than the visitor; that the institution existed for things rather than for human beings."

These ideas, like similar successful civic reforms, were then considered revolutionary, and advocates of them were looked upon as radicals. The popularization of museums was a new idea and was considered unscientific by some of the American Museum staff. To have a great crowd come to the museum, as they had to see uranium minerals containing the newly discovered radium, was considered vulgar. The egos of various staff members were shaken by the dictum that the exhibits were the important thing and should hold the spotlight, and the director's idea that the glamorization of the exhibits was more important than the glorification of the curators was openly resented by some members of his scientific staff.

His board of trustees, it must be remembered, was composed of New York's successful financiers. To be associated with things scientific was pleasing to them, and they either did not appreciate or else heartily disapproved of the sentiment Director Bumpus had expressed in placing the phrases *For the people* and *For education* before the phrase *For science* on the museum bookplate. The caption under another fullpage picture in the July 1908 number of *World's Work*, reading "Hermon C. Bumpus, Director of the American Museum of Natural History in New York, who is using it as a great instrument to reach the masses of the people," struck a sour note with certain members of both the scientific staff and the board of trustees. They were not at all interested in being associated with the masses. It was the era when the phrase "The public be damned" was popular in certain quarters.

On January 22, 1908, Morris K. Jesup died. In all institutions where the chief executive has held his office for a long time his passing is sure to initiate changes in the organization. The American Museum of Natural History proved no exception to the rule. The authority that had gradually been vested in the office of director was substantially reduced, and as soon as another position was available Dr. Bumpus resigned.

He felt that his ideas about popular education had been repudiated and that he had lost the respect of men of science because of the imagined failure of his museum work. He was deeply discouraged but not despondent. For a time he abandoned museum work and scientific associations to accept a position as business manager of the University of Wisconsin. By hard work in new surroundings, he hoped to overcome his discouragement.

One who appreciates Dr. Bumpus' feelings when he was forced to leave the museum can well understand the significance of a brief notation he wrote thirty-one years later on the Henry W. Kent Diploma, which was conferred on him by the American Association of Museums at a notable gathering in Columbus, Ohio, on May 17, 1941, with the governor of Ohio and other dignitaries in attendance. Dr. Clark Wissler, president of the association, concluded his presentation speech, in which he traced the life history and achievements of Dr. Bumpus, by saying: "It is in recognition of these many achievements and of your effective leadership in education in the museum way that the American Association of Museums presents you with this diploma. By this act the Association seeks to honor you by awarding this token of merit known as the HENRY W. KENT DIPLOMA, in memory of Anne Lamont Flagler, which reads, 'In recognition of distinguished service rendered to the cause of museum education.'"

Dr. Bumpus, deeply moved, carefully wrote in his fine hand along the margin of the diploma, "More appreciated than any other testimonial. H. C. B." His ideas had been vindicated.

CHAPTER VI

Friend to the Gaekwar of Baroda

His Highness the Gaekwar of Baroda, in Gujarat, India, was reputed to be one of the world's richest men, so wealthy that not even he had much idea of his total fortune. He was the possessor also of magnificent and enormous gems, including carpets made of pearls. De Witt MacKenzie of the *Baltimore Sun* wrote: "I saw the Gaekwar competing in robes and jewels with two score other great princes one night at a viceregal reception, and my eyesight hasn't been the same since." The stairs to the royal palace were flanked by gold cannons.

Nevertheless, despite his great wealth the Gaekwar was one of the most progressive of Indian princes and had introduced many civil reforms into his country. Seeking to modernize it further and to provide greater comfort for his two million subjects, he came to America in 1906. Since he was interested in education it was not unnatural that in the course of his tour he called on Morris K. Jesup and asked to be shown the American Museum of Natural History. Mr. Jesup introduced him to Dr. Bumpus. The Gaekwar's close association with Dr. Bumpus in the years that followed, though extraordinary, was not surprising to those who knew either of the men. Whether it was the richest man in the world or a poor artist or a student, if he had something constructive to offer, Dr. Bumpus was interested and anxious to help him. He soon became the Gaekwar's most intimate friend, and Baroda's special representative, in America.

Quick to appreciate His Highness' liberal ideas, Dr. Bumpus sent many young Americans to Baroda, among them Ralph C. Whitnach, a Brown alumnus of the class of 1906, who founded the first bank in Baroda, installed its free compulsory school system, and built factories, model tenements, and dairy farms.

When the Gaekwar died in 1939 the *Baltimore Evening Sun*, under the caption "A Friend of Britain, a Father to My People," had this to say of him:

England has lost a loyal friend and a great stabilizing influence in her Indian Empire through the death in Bombay of the 75-year-old Gaekwar of Baroda—one of the most powerful of Hindustan's Arabian Nights princes. It is a loss that Britain could ill afford in these days when millions of nationalists are challenging her sovereignty over India in their drive for independence.

The Gaekwar, despite his fabulous wealth and his power of life and death over his two million and a half subjects, was a man of the people. He was a half century ahead of his time in a backward India which in many respects still moves drowsily.

All his long reign of sixty-four years was spent as a labor of love for his subjects. He recognized and remedied ills which in various other sections of India have led to the growth of the demand for *puran Swaraj*—absolute independence.

Perhaps he brought the seed of his broad humanitarianism with him when, as a tiny lad, he was fetched to the gilded marble palace and golden throne from his native mountains, where he had been a humble shepherd boy. He had known the pinch of want. For the Gaekwar, while of the royal blood, belonged to a poor branch of the family and came to rule through a quirk of fate which pointed to him when the Maharajah was deposed.

His creed was well summed up in a letter quoted three years ago by the *Times of India*. Writing to a friend His Highness said: "My policy has been to be a friend to the British Government, to be a father to my people, and to safeguard the dignity, rights, and self-respect of the state and its ruler."

The Gaekwar's oldest son had been educated in the public schools of England and at Oxford. The British government at this time, by making it legally easy to collect debts from the Indian princes, encouraged the merchants and moneylenders of England to extend liberal credit to the sons of these rulers. The natural result was that these young men, placed in a foreign land with limitless credit, were inclined to dissipation, since there was someone at every turn to encourage it.

His oldest son had succumbed to these temptations while he was at Oxford, and the Gaekwar was determined to prevent the same thing happening to his second son, who was graduated from Harrow in 1906. Sending the boy to America to finish his education, the Gaekwar asked Dr. Bumpus to assume guardianship. Little realizing how difficult a task he was assuming, Dr. Bumpus consented.

On the afternoon of Prince Jasingrao's arrival at Dr. Bumpus' home in New Rochelle, Carey Bumpus and the neighborhood boys were finishing off the last few layers of brick on the top of the chimney of a new clubhouse. After introducing the newcomer to the gang as "Jay Gaekwar," Carey gave him a bucketful of mortar to carry up the chimney to the boys who were setting the bricks. Jasingrao was a good sport; he decided that if American boys had their fun in this way he would tag along. Unfortunately his education as a prince had included the use of his hands only for sports, and to convey a bucketful of cement on his shoulder up a ladder was more than he could manage. The cement slopped over on his clothes and down his neck, and his suit was ruined. When his baggage arrived, however, it was evident that the damage was of little moment, for he had thirty-four other suits.

The entrance requirements at Harvard were so at variance with those of Cambridge University, for which Prince Jasingrao had prepared, that it was necessary for him to attend an American preparatory school for two years. Since Carey Bumpus was then attending Horace Mann High School in New York City, it was natural that Jay, who was of the same age, should join him. From then on the prince, who was small in stature, weighed less than a hundred pounds, and had the dark olive complexion of the East Indian, was known as Carey Bumpus' shadow. He was a better than average athlete and particularly good at soccer and tennis. His scholastic standing was that of the average American boy of his age.

The guardianship of the prince was not too difficult during the two years he was in preparatory school, for the two boys got along well together and Jasingrao's allowance was no greater than that of any of his companions. However, it was noticed that he was very careless with his personal jewelry, of which he had a considerable amount in the way of diamond stickpins, platinum and pearl cuff links, and a very fine Swiss watch and chain. He was forever losing one article or another, and when he claimed to have lost a beautiful diamond stickpin with a pearl pendant on the football field in Rochelle Park, where the Bumpuses lived, Mrs. Bumpus spent several hours in a fruitless search for it. As it turned out, the article in question had found its way to a pawnbroker's shop, along with the other missing items. The prince was picking up American ways very rapidly.

He soon found a still easier way to augment his income. He would suggest that it would be worth while educationally for him to visit some distant historical spot, preferably in one of the larger cities, during a vacation. Departing with adequate funds for the trip, he would telegraph Dr. Bumpus soon after arrival that he was out of money. Since it was hardly feasible to leave the son of one of the world's richest men destitute in a strange city, Western Union would be called upon to disburse more funds.

The prince worked this trick once too often and Dr. Bumpus decided that he must have a companion. Carey had served the purpose while both were attending high school, but Carey was going to his father's alma mater, while Jasingrao was destined for Harvard. So Dr. Bumpus appointed William Spicer, a Brown graduate then studying at the Harvard Law School, to steer the young prince through his freshman year at Harvard. His reward for his services was a trip to India with the young prince during the following summer vacation.

At the beginning of the prince's sophomore year, the authorities at Harvard felt that it would be more to his interest to room with a football athlete than with a graduate law student, and arrangements were made for him to do so. They made no attempt, however, to provide the prince with social contacts in Boston or in Cambridge. Possibly it would have been wasted effort, but in any event, the prince, lacking such contacts, soon found others at the stage door, and rapidly followed in his brother's footsteps.

However, he maintained his scholastic standing and received a degree from Harvard. It was then necessary for Dr. Bumpus to evacuate him, by way of Springfield and the Cunard Line, under an alias, for Boston merchants of a certain type, like their English brethren, had learned that the credit of a rich man's son is excellent. They were waiting for him at the South Station in Boston when he was boarding the New York train in Springfield.

Bumpus' ingenuity went even further in getting the young man back to India. It was useless to give him traveler's checks for they would be gambled away before the ship reached port and the cables would be hot with undeniable requests for more funds. To circumvent such happenings Dr. Bumpus requested Thomas Cook & Son to have a thousand dollars waiting for the young graduate at each of their agencies from New York to Bombay. Like a hen picking up pieces of grain that lead through the chicken-yard gate, Jasingrao picked up his funds on his homeward trek.

On January 30, 1912, the Gaekwar wrote to Dr. Bumpus from his palace in Baroda:

MY DEAR DR. BUMPUS:

I hope this letter will find you, Mrs. Bumpus, and your son well and happy.

Jasingrao after his serious accident from a horse block is doing well, though he is advised to do no work, which I think he likes. My other son who had an accident in Oxford is now in India and is doing well. My daughter's marriage which was to come off with Maharajah Scundia had to be abandoned as she changed her mind at the last moment. The marriage was brought about at her own request and against family advice, though there were few young men to choose from who were not married. In India, owing to caste system, the choice is unfortunately limited.

I should be glad to hear from you at times. . . .

I am sending you a frame which I hope you will accept as a mark of my regard for you and for what you have done for Jasingrao.

Your sincere friend,
COYAJI RAO GAEKWAR

The Gaekwar evidently understood that, whatever the results, Dr. Bumpus had done his best for Jasingrao.

When funds were being sought for the new Harvard Medical School dormitory, a notice of Prince Jasingrao's death in Holland appeared in the American papers. In a letter of sympathy to His Highness, Dr. Bumpus' elder son, then a graduate of the Harvard Medical School, suggested that it would be fitting for the Gaekwar to endow a room in the new building in memory of his son's stay in America and his education at Harvard. The Gaekwar was favorably impressed with this idea and furnished the funds for the memorial.

CHAPTER VII

University Administrator

WISCONSIN 1911-1914   TUFTS 1915-1919

TEN years as director of the American Museum of Natural History, with its ample budgets and generous appropriations from both the municipal and state governments, had given Dr. Bumpus considerable experience not only in handling large sums of public money but also in dealing with legislators and lesser politicians. He had been impressed by the methods of a reformed Tammany. He had expected his New England conscience and upbringing to lead him into clashes with Wigwam members and was surprised when he encountered no difficulties with them. One of the chieftains, realizing that Dr. Bumpus was a newcomer to New York and would be responsible for disbursing large sums of public money, told him not to hesitate to fire any Tammany appointee who proved incompetent; all Tammany asked and expected was that while they were in power their supporters should receive preference on the public payroll. For their own interests, he added, they would see to it that people were supplied who were capable of filling the positions. A Tammany alderman explained to Dr. Bumpus that if he ever wanted to enlarge the museum Tammany would be delighted to assist in procuring the needed funds, for their specialty was obtaining and disbursing public funds.

In the meantime the University of Wisconsin, noted for its progressive ideas, had been growing so rapidly that President Van Hise found much of his time taken up with its expanding business affairs and the procurement of new appropriations from the state legislature, and in consequence had little time to devote to the academic program and the faculty. He wished to find someone familiar with university needs and organization who had been accustomed also to manage large public funds and who understood the methods of legislators. The position involved the handling of an annual budget of three million dollars, the expenditure of which the governor of the state had entrusted to a board of regents. The budget and the funds it represented were in considerable confusion when Dr. Bumpus took over.

Other duties of the business manager were to see that the new buildings then being constructed met the specifications, that physical accommodations were available for the ever-expanding departments of the rapidly growing university, and that the maintenance and heating of the physical plant of the university were adequate. Moreover, he was expected to prepare financial reports for President Van Hise and the board of regents when new appropriations from the state were required.

This was the first such office established by an American university, and there was no precedent to go by. Nor did the fields in which Dr. Bumpus had distinguished himself—teaching, biology, and museum work—give him any direct help in his new work. However, President Van Hise had faith and confidence in the man he had chosen, and Bumpus went directly at the unusual job with his accustomed vigor and resourcefulness.

How diversified and comprehensive were the duties of the new office is best shown by two incidents that occurred while he held it.

The department of music had guaranteed one of the nation's best symphony orchestras a large sum for a concert at the university gymnasium, but the ticket sale failed to cover the guarantee by several thousand dollars. The state legislature, which in the agricultural state of Wisconsin was made up largely of hardheaded farmers, was not spending state money for symphony concerts, no matter how famous the orchestra was. How was the university to get out of this dilemma? The resourceful business manager applied his biometric methods, and they worked. The orchestra contract called for 140 musicians. By careful count it was found that only 130 had appeared, and that the contract had therefore not been met. Thus the university's funds were preserved.

The other incident might have had more serious consequences. A prowler entered one of the sorority houses at night and escaped undetected. The incident was repeated, the university was in an uproar, and parents were sending for their daughters to return home. A firm of nationally known detectives was employed and at last reported that the culprit had been spotted. In shadowing him they had seen him accompany one of the sorority girls to a roadhouse not far from the city and there spend the better part of the night. The man had not too good a reputation in the city, and the evidence of his guilt seemed conclusive. All that was necessary for his arrest was the business manager's assent. Again Dr. Bumpus' biological training asserted itself. Before facts in science can be reported all evidence must be scrupulously examined. He visited the roadhouse where the midnight seduction was alleged to have occurred and found it to be the home of the coed's aunt, where the girl had often spent weekends.

In the business office Dr. Bumpus reduced the financial chaos he had found to law and order, and he introduced new methods of accounting that would more quickly give a picture of what the various departments of the university were costing the state. Nonetheless, he was undoubtedly glad, at the end of three years, to resign his unique position and accept the presidency of Tufts College, to return to an occupation more in keeping with his experience and training.

He had made a pleasant group of friends during his stay in Madison and left behind him an atmosphere of mutual respect. At the time of his resignation President Henry S.

HERMON CAREY BUMPUS

Pritchett of the Carnegie Foundation for the Advancement of Teaching wrote him the following letter of appreciation:

MY DEAR DR. BUMPUS:

I have been looking over with very great interest your report for the year ending June 30, 1912, upon the receipts and expenditures of the University of Wisconsin for the biennial period. It is one of the most illuminating and interesting financial statements that have come under my eye. I feel, of course, very much pleased with the use which has been made of our bulletin, and quite agree with you that the summaries of expenditures on pages 62 and 63 make a most valuable addition to such an exhibit. They show, in fact, on two pages a general view of the expenditures and their distribution which gives to the eye at once a financial picture of what has gone on. I want to congratulate you upon the admirable statement which you have issued. If we could have such a view as this gives of the expenditures of every institution, we should soon make steps in education which will require a long time, I fear, to make without it.

Very sincerely yours,
HENRY S. PRITCHETT

January 3, 1913

Of Dr. Bumpus' work at the University of Wisconsin the president of the board of regents, James F. Trautman, wrote: "Since the office of business manager had just been created, the organization and development pertaining to the work of the office required special attention on the part of the regents and unusual energy, care, and discretion on the part of the new business manager. I am glad to say that Dr. Bumpus met his duties with the enthusiasm of a scholar and the thoroughness of a vigorous business man. Owing to the peculiar demands made upon the business administration of our university in the course of the last three years for all kinds of business data and information, the work of the business office was made exceedingly difficult. But for Dr. Bumpus's tactfulness, diligence, and efficiency, much confusion might have resulted. His experience at the university will undoubtedly be of great help to him in the new work he is about to undertake. The position of President of Tufts

College will open a field to Dr. Bumpus's energies and capacity which is peculiarly suited to him. When Dr. Bumpus leaves Madison he takes with him the best wishes and highest regard of every member of the Board of Regents."

While Dr. Bumpus was being considered as a candidate for the presidency of Tufts two letters in particular, among the many sent to the authorities in advocation of his selection, seem to typify the admiration and respect which educators felt for Dr. Bumpus and his work. Each is far from being the perfunctory recommendation usual on such an occasion.

E. Benjamin Andrews, former president of Brown University, wrote: "Absolutely nothing could be said too favorable for Dr. Bumpus. The only question for Tufts to raise is, can he be had? As an administrator, teacher, scholar, disciplinarian, and all the other characters, he is all that could be desired in the head of a modern college. While scholarly and a prince of teachers, he is a gifted man of affairs. He knows men, young and old, and commands them. As for begging power, when money is to be raised, he out-cheeks the Sphinx. Bumpus has also the gift of growth. He is ambitious for himself and for every cause he espouses. There could not be a better man for the head of Tufts for the simple reason that God doesn't produce any better.

"In looking over the above, I notice that I have failed to emphasize Bumpus's extraordinary originality in doing things. He has his own way in approaching tasks, and it is nearly always the wise and telling way."

William Morton Wheeler, professor of economic entomology at Harvard, prophetically wrote in part: "Professor Bumpus combines, in a very extraordinary manner, abilities which taken singly would make any one man a great success in life. He has not only a thorough university training as an investigator, so that he is able to appreciate the value of work done by teachers and students in any single branch of knowledge, but has also a very penetrating insight into human nature and a wide knowledge and experience of men, rarely found among university men, combined with an extraordinary capacity for executive and purely routine business work. All of these abilities have been manifested to an unusual degree throughout his whole career. He not only has the ability to select men able to cooperate with him, but is also able to induce them to work with one another in the most enthusiastic and serviceable manner. In other words, he is a master not only in stimulating cooperation in his human environment, but in getting good 'teamwork' out of all the men he may select to carry out a particular program. He is possessed of unusual originality and ingenuity in overcoming difficulties and in suggesting lines of endeavor serviceable to science and to the community in which he lives. He has magnetic personality and of such a character that all students and teachers who come in contact with him not only admire him but acquire a great affection for him. . . . Any educational institution that secures the services of Professor Bumpus is greatly to be congratulated. I know of no man who could so quickly and skillfully increase the efficiency of a college and make it fulfill its great function toward the community which it is destined to serve."

Dr. Bumpus' inaugural address, "The Obligation of the Trustees, Faculty, and Alumni to the College," revealed the new president as a man keenly conscious of the responsibility of office, in no wise misled by the vanity of power, and determined so to use his authority that it should indeed keep faith with those who had given it to him.

The problem before him was well outlined in an editorial in the *Boston Transcript*: "The whole college—students, professors, and alumni—was becoming restless under the suspense entailed by two years of apparent inactivity. Professor Hooper, as acting president since the resignation of President Frederick W. Hamilton, was both popular and efficient, but no matter how valuable his efforts may have been, there was too much administrative uncertainty to allow the college to make any distinct progress.

UNIVERSITY ADMINISTRATOR

"Now that this uncertainty has been relieved, the forward march should at once be begun. The burden which Dr. Bumpus is about to assume is far from easy, and is of such a nature as to call into play all the business ability which he is reputed to possess. Tufts in some respects is an overgrown college. From an educational standpoint it is really a university. To the original arts department have been added several professional schools, all of which continue to impose such a severe strain on the institution's treasury that Tufts has on hand a financial problem of no mean proportions. It is not overstating the facts to say that the college at this very minute needs an expansion fund of $1,000,000 and as large a sum for additional endowment. New buildings are urgently required, faculty salaries must be raised to a decent level, and some additions to the teaching staff made. To effect all these improvements will undoubtedly be the first task to which the new president will devote himself. And in this work he will have the undivided support of all friends of the college.

"One thing seems to be reasonably sure. Dr. Bumpus must be going into the affair with his eyes wide open. A two years' open search for a president has at least had the effect of acquainting the world with the full extent of the financial problem facing the college."

In analyzing the problem at Tufts, President Bumpus first made a study of the number of boys and girls of grammar, high school, and college age in the state in relation to the location of his institution. He found that by far the larger proportion of the approximately 318,000 boys and girls between the ages of eighteen and twenty-two in the state of Massachusetts centered about Boston, but that only 12,000 of them were attending college.

Then why was it, he asked himself, that in spite of the number of available students there were so few actually in college? There were three reasons, he found: first, cost; second, entrance requirements; and third, the student's delay in making a decision as to his lifework. Dr. Bumpus proposed to attack these barriers at once.

On March 9, 1916, the first annual report of the new regime appeared. President Bumpus reported that the enrollment had increased 25 per cent, that the entrance requirements had been liberalized, and that the college was doing everything possible to plan its work to meet the requirements of private and public schools. "The educational staff has been strengthened," he wrote, "and the physical equipment improved. The alumni are taking an increased interest in the welfare of the college and there have been an encouraging number of gifts.

"We have paid our bills and closed the year without deficit. There are twice as many students in the School of Liberal Arts as there were in 1910. The attendance at the Dental School—an increase of 40 per cent—has forced us to consider the advisability of advancing the entrance requirements or limiting the classes. According to the report of the Finance Committee, our total capital improvement during the year has been approximately $250,000 and our total endowment, exclusive of educational buildings and grounds, now equals $2,200,000. In a list of 311 of the leading colleges and universities there are 277 with an endowment inferior to ours."

The *Boston Evening Transcript* made the following editorial comment on the report: "Good things were expected of President Bumpus when he came to take the leadership of Tufts, and good things are evidenced of him by the facts of his first annual report as now issued. The college has paid its bills and closed the year without a deficit, an achievement seldom equaled in the history of Tufts, or, for that matter, of any college. This favorable showing must, however, be taken exclusively for itself, and not interpreted to mean that all of Tufts' financial problems are solved. The college still stands badly in need of funds. President Bumpus proposed to get these funds, but he believes before a college makes an appeal, it should first make itself worthy. He has had wide experience in the business management of a college, and he has turned it to good use in order to set the House of Tufts in entire order. He is also striving to broaden the institution's constituency. When he has done these things, certainly much of the road towards assurance of larger endowment will have been traveled already. In this policy of insistence that a college should pay as it goes, Mr. Bumpus is in accord with President Murlin of Boston University. Nearly all other college presidents differ, holding that the only way to achieve expansion is to expand, and let the size of the need at the end of the year be stimulus to the size of the support which friends of the institution, seeing the need, will be called on to give it. We have no purpose here to impugn the wisdom of this policy. It often produces great results. But when a college, needing money as Tufts does, completes the year with all bills paid and no deficit, it is time to give its president hearty congratulations."

The new president's insight into human nature and his sympathetic personality were soon discovered by students as well as faculty. The fact that the president's black-and-white setter always followed him into chapel and slept on the rostrum during the service was an expression of his character that the younger generation appreciated at once.

A first-year medical student who had been eliminated for failure to measure up to academic standards sought an interview with the president and told him that his parents had deprived themselves for years to accumulate sufficient funds to send him to medical school and would be heartbroken to learn that their sacrifice had been in vain. President Bumpus explained to the youth that failure as a medical student was no indication of failure in other fields but simply meant that he had been misplaced. He went on to say that inasmuch as the college had accepted him as a student and now found he was not adequate for such training, they would return his tuition fee. The boy could hardly believe his ears. "You mean you will give me my money back?" "Certainly," said

Dr. Bumpus. "You paid in advance for an education that you are not to receive. Why should the college keep the money when it hasn't delivered the goods?"

Years later when Dr. Bumpus required some plumbing fixtures for one of the early American houses he had remodeled as summer residences at Duxbury he found them advertised by one of the largest supply houses in Boston. When he went to purchase them the owner inquired, "Aren't you Dr. Bumpus?" When the answer was affirmative he said, "You did me the greatest favor any man ever did another. You saved me from being a poor doctor and gave me the chance I needed to be a successful merchant." From that time on all supplies for Dr. Bumpus' various Duxbury houses were furnished at wholesale prices—a mark of real appreciation.

At about this time an incident took place that Bumpus afterward enjoyed relating. An automobile accident occurred just in front of the president's house, and someone came rushing to the front door and told the maid that the doctor was wanted at once. Dr. Bumpus, in his study nearby, heard her reply, "Ah, and for sure, he's a doctor all right, but he's that kind of a doctor that's no use to nobody."

At the time of Dr. Bumpus' death President Leonard Carmichael of Tufts wrote to Professor A. D. Mead of Brown University: "Certainly the period of Bumpus's presidency was a fruitful and important one for this college. . . . His years at Tufts were years very much like the present. They were all years during which the world was at war, and his opportunity to develop his ideas and ideals for higher education were naturally gravely interfered with by the condition of the world as a whole in the period between 1914 and 1918. . . .

"During the period of the organization of the Student Army Training Corps at Tufts College, Dr. Bumpus divided his time between the campus and Washington. As a result, Tufts was one of the first institutions to start proper preparations for the Student's Army Training Corps, and the records of the college show that in the judgment of the War Department the SATC at Tufts College was one of the most effectively administered in America."

The trips to Washington to which President Carmichael referred were in connection with Dr. Bumpus' personal contribution to the war effort. He had found work in the Transportation Division of the Quartermaster Corps, where he could exercise his administrative abilities. His task was to organize camps for the training of truck drivers and to arrange for the crating and shipping of their trucks to Europe. Under his dynamic leadership three teams were formed, each crating up thirty-three trucks in eight-hour shifts. In order to make it an even hundred a day there was keen rivalry among the teams to see which would get a thirty-fourth truck aboard the transport.

Dr. Bumpus was offered a commission as major, but it seemed to him that with his younger son in the Reserve Officers' Training Corps and his older son in the Army Medical Corps some member of the family should be free to act independently in case of a family emergency. Moreover, the work he had set out to do at Tufts was not completed, and he felt that he was more urgently needed there.

By the war's end, however, he had, in his opinion, accomplished what he had set out to do at Tufts. He had made the college a going concern and had seen it safely and successfully through the critical days of the war. He was now fifty-seven years old. Throughout his life his enthusiasm for the task in hand had left him little opportunity to pursue his personal interests, and now he longed for freedom from heavy responsibilities. So he resigned the presidency of Tufts College at the end of 1918.

A final summary of Dr. Bumpus' work at Tufts is to be found in the *Tufts College Graduate* for December 1918: "The announcement of the resignation of President Hermon C. Bumpus came with rather startling suddenness to most

Tufts men and to the college world in general. That a college or any institution intent upon the maintenance of a definitely expanding policy should be compelled frequently to change its chief administrative officer is a misfortune. That Tufts should, in this year of educational, national, and international crises, lose the services of the leader who has taken the college so loyally and successfully through the crisis of the war and who has so many educational ideals for the future is a double misfortune. . . .

"The work of successfully administering the affairs of Tufts College during the past four years has not been easy. The problem of adjusting any college to war conditions and the readjustment to the conditions of the new day, and all within a few months, is a task that at the outset would have seemed well-nigh impossible; yet all of these Dr. Bumpus has accomplished with credit to the institution and to the nation which he and the college have served.

"Confronted at the outset with the task of avoiding the annual financial deficit, from which Professor Hooper had temporarily saved the college, he met the situation successfully year by year, without checking the growth of the college in numbers or in usefulness to the community. . . . With the sudden ending of the war, and the hasty demobilization of the Student Army Training Corps, he met the changed conditions with reorganization plans so attractive that Tufts has more students on the Hill today than ever before in its history.

"That Dr. Bumpus has won a place in the hearts of Tufts graduates was impressively demonstrated at the National Tufts Night of the Boston Club. That he has high standing in the community and in the educational world is attested by the honors that have been given him and by the many opportunities that have come to him to serve upon committees and with organizations of all sorts. Perhaps not the least significant and enduring feature of his educational policy is the more liberal college entrance requirements which Tufts

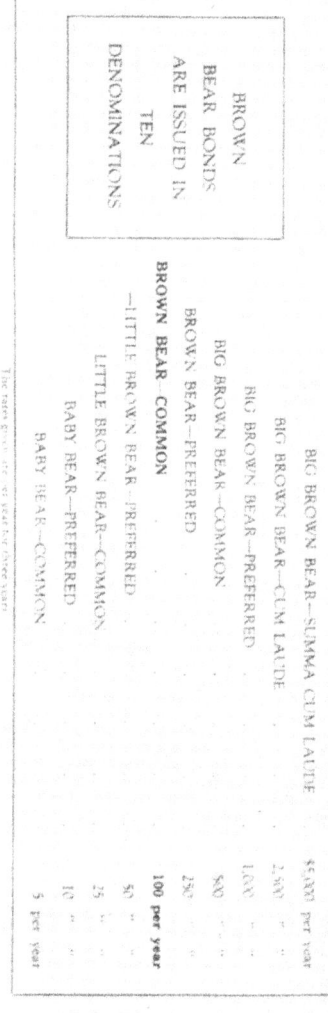
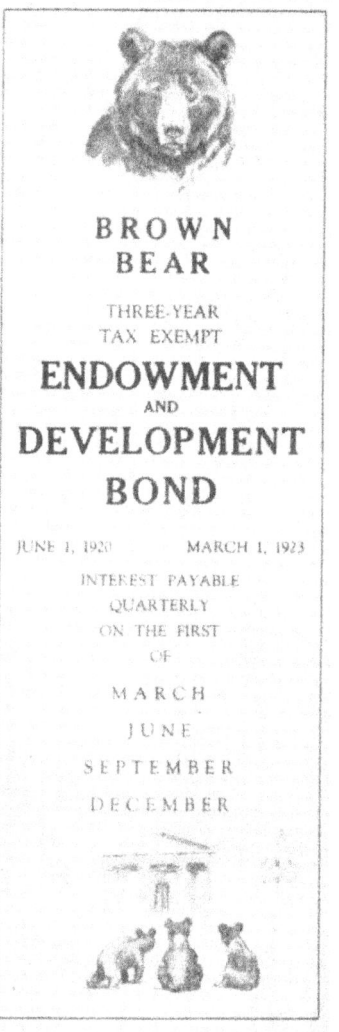

The Brown Bear bonds, a Bumpus idea, brought contributions to Brown University's endowment drive

There were Little Brown Bear bonds, too

The trailside museum, now familiar to all national park tourists, was originated by Bumpus

The natural history shrine—another educational device conceived by Bumpus

has adopted under his administration. Only those closely in touch with secondary education can appreciate the full significance of the Tufts 'Free Marginal Group' which makes it possible for a student to present for college admission any subject in which he is proficient. All in all, his administration has been characterized by progressiveness, breadth of view, soundness of judgment, and sincerity. We appreciate his services and regret his departure."

CHAPTER VIII

Builder and Gardener

THOUGH Dr. Bumpus never criticized others for indulging in such sports as golf and tennis, and on the contrary was always active in support of public playgrounds, he was himself incapable of enjoying any exercise or recreation that was not constructive. Something material and usable must result from his recreation.

Plants and flowers, birds and trees were a constant source of enjoyment to him. He invariably kept a little grain in his room and would sprinkle it outside the door or window to attract the birds. This he did almost to the last day of his life in California, where he derived particular pleasure from the many mourning doves that gathered around his door. It was natural therefore that he hated cats. Throughout their married life his wife would tell her friends that she could never understand why all her cats disappeared or were stepped on by the horse in the stable.

The actual care of a garden was too routine a matter to give him enjoyment, but to plan and lay out a garden was a recurring source of pleasure to him, and if it could be unusual in design or location he was delighted.

However, his creative and artistic instincts found their greatest stimulation in building. During his lifetime he either built or supervised the remodeling of more than twenty houses. His first venture in unusual building was the refashioning of the Philippine exhibition hall at the St. Louis Exposition into a summer home on the shore of Long Island Sound. While he was in St. Louis arranging for the transportation of the Philippine exhibit to the American Museum of Natural History, the fair buildings were being auctioned off for their value as secondhand material. With his characteristic ability for sensing utility in the unusual he purchased the Philippine hall with the idea of turning it into a summer cottage.

It was then necessary for him to find a place to erect the building, for by the time he returned to New York it was already being torn down and placed on freight cars for shipment. Dr. Bumpus spent the next few weekends bicycling along the Connecticut shore with his son, looking for a suitable location, and finally found one at Westport, on Long Island Sound. The surprise of the residents when, instead of the orthodox summer cottage, a typical Philippine bungalow arose can well be imagined. The tradespeople never had to inquire where the Bumpus family lived, for the house became one of the local points of interest, like the hill not far away where Putnam had been chased by the Indians.

Carpenters were employed to erect the framework of the building, which was some seventy-five feet long by fifty feet wide, but the interior and exterior covering were constructed by Dr. Bumpus and his son. The outside of the house was covered with bamboo matting arranged in attractive squares and held in place by poles of the same material. The interior was divided by split bamboo partitions running up only seven feet, and from this point to the ceiling were hung nets and various decorative South Sea mats. Privacy was sacrificed for art, for anyone in any room could talk in the softest tones and yet be easily heard anywhere in the house. It was a worth-while sacrifice, however, for a more enjoyable or cooler summer cottage would be difficult to produce. The fireplace mantel was made from huge tropical shells, three of them serving not only as decoration but also as storage space. Much of the furniture, made of materials from the South Seas, was constructed by Dr. Bumpus and his son. A fair idea of the appearance of the interior may be gained from the present beachcomber night clubs, except that space and light were substituted for the congestion and darkness of the clubs.

Westport was only an hour's ride from New York on the New Haven Railroad, and Dr. Bumpus found a swim in the salt water of Long Island Sound the best type of relaxation after a hard day's work in New York. His family enjoyed the Westport summer home too. Here young Carey and Prince Jasingrao of Baroda learned to sail, and later, in their college years, they found the Philippine bungalow an ideal spot for many an enjoyable house party during vacations.

When the family had been living in New England for several years and both boys had been graduated from the Harvard Medical School, Dr. Bumpus' love for flowers led him to place in a northern setting a house of an architectural plan more usual in the tropics. On a suitable lot in Waban, a pleasant suburb of Boston, he built a small Italian villa, with a glassed-in patio where flowers could be enjoyed throughout the long New England winters. A Mediterranean-type house in New England, with its rigorous climate, was unusual, and the originality and charm of the house attracted considerable attention. Mrs. Jack Gardner's palace on the Fenway attempted a similar plan on a magnificent scale, and Boston artisans are still called upon to stop the inevitable leaks resulting from snow, ice, and freezing in both these houses, orphaned from their natural setting.

To build a house in the customary way, with blueprints and under contract, did not appeal to Dr. Bumpus. He had no interest in such an undertaking. When Mrs. Bumpus, who had also caught the building fever, constructed summer houses in Duxbury under an architect's supervision and with contractual labor, her husband's only interest was in naming them. Appropriately enough, he often gave them the names of shore birds. His wife's first venture, a three-room affair built on the beach, he called "Peep."

BUILDER AND GARDENER

During the family's last year of residence in Madison, Wisconsin, an elderly aunt and uncle of Mrs. Bumpus had died in Dorchester, Massachusetts, just a few weeks apart. Their home was filled with rather nice early American furniture, the disposal of which presented a considerable problem, for it was not advisable to leave it in a rented house. Interest in his family history had familiarized Dr. Bumpus with the town of Duxbury, just across the bay from Plymouth, and he solved the problem by purchasing an old Cape Cod house, badly in need of repair, on Duxbury Bay. The furniture was moved to this house, and he and Mrs. Bumpus returned to Madison. The fact that he neglected to lock the door made little difference in this honest community, which retains many of its original Puritan traits. When he returned East to assume the presidency of Tufts, everything at Duxbury was just as he had left it, despite the open door.

The basement of the Cape Cod house had been used, before he acquired it, as a place for slaughtering pigs, and when an unusually large one was slaughtered its picture and weight were drawn in chalk on the blackened beams. Dr. Bumpus, placing French doors and windows in the wall facing the sea, made of the basement a very attractive dining room in which the pictorial pigs were retained as a decorative feature.

The remodeling of this cottage had proved a great source of relaxation to Dr. Bumpus, and its sale, at a considerable profit because of the artistic improvements, supplied the capital for further ventures in house-building.

In carrying out his hobby Dr. Bumpus was fortunate to have as his associate Chester Bates, one of New England's unusual characters, a jack-of-all-trades who became his constant companion in the work of building and rebuilding houses. Dr. Bumpus' only worry in this companionship was that Chester's salty profanity might creep into his own speech when he was leading chapel as president of Tufts or sitting with the Board of Fellows at Brown University—an unnecessary worry, as it happened, for those who worked closest to him never heard him utter a word of profanity, however great the provocation.

Together the two moved and rebuilt an old farmhouse they discovered some seventeen miles inland from Duxbury. During its two hundred or more years of existence the sides of the house had fallen in and the living room and kitchen had become a passageway for the cattle in the adjoining pasture. After taking the house apart Dr. Bumpus and Chester moved it down to the shore of Duxbury Bay in one of the first Ford station wagons that ever rambled the byways of that region. After restoring the house and installing all modern conveniences, they named it "Plover." Here all Dr. Bumpus' grandchildren spent their summers, and they became so fond of Duxbury that Dr. Bumpus presented to his eldest grandson, on his twenty-first birthday, another house that he and Chester had built.

After acquiring this shore property, situated on some high land overlooking the town, Dr. Bumpus discovered that the land had been a pasture on the farm belonging to his ancestor, Edouard Bon Passe, who had moved from Plymouth to Duxbury early in the seventeenth century. Since the founder of the family had been a Huguenot, Dr. Bumpus tried to name the place "Huguenot Hill." It had been a cow pasture, however, with a brush shelter on the crest to give the animals shade, and so the place had become known locally as "Cow Tent Hill." So picturesque a name could not readily be displaced, and as Cow Tent Hill it is still known to the local residents.

Dr. Bumpus was proud that no professional artisans had been employed in the construction of either of these Duxbury houses; the plumbing, wiring, papering, painting, and even the cabinetwork had all been done by Chester and himself. It was while he was plastering one of the houses that some tourists stopped to inquire the direction to Plymouth Rock, and, thinking him an unusually intelligent plasterer, asked what he did in his spare time. He replied that he acted as a college president when he was not plastering. At the next filling station the travelers told the attendant that they had met a nice old plasterer who thought he was a college president, and they wondered why the Duxbury authorities had not committed him.

A little later Dr. Bumpus conceived the idea of building a house out of materials usually thrown away, such as slab sides of logs, which the local mill burned. On Cow Tent Hill he cut down a number of cedar trees and from them constructed one of his most artistic cottages. Situated in the yard of an old New England farmhouse he had restored, it made an ideal guest house.

While carrying on these enjoyable labors in Duxbury he was also making repeated trips to Washington, where he had become interested in the work of the American Red Cross and the development of its museum. Under his guidance and inspiration, and with the help of artists and sculptors, a number of miniature groups were installed, depicting the work of the Red Cross as carried on both in wartime and in civilian disasters.

Returning from a trip to New York, Bumpus chanced to meet on the train his old friend President Faunce of Brown University, who expressed considerable anxiety about a much needed endowment for the university. The first thing Bumpus knew he found himself enlisted heart and soul in the campaign to raise three million dollars. Although he had planned to spend that winter in Florida, he gave up his vacation in favor of another hard job that needed doing. It was exactly the kind of thing that Dr. Bumpus could not resist, particularly when it concerned the welfare of his beloved alma mater.

He took over the organization of the drive for funds, and though he kept himself in the background he so inspired his chosen helpers that Thomas B. Appleget, vice-president of the Rockefeller Foundation, wrote of his efforts: "My first intimate contact with him was in the university's campaign for three million dollars in increased endowment. Then for the first time I saw the man's energy, his endless ingenuity, his courage and his optimism. I had already been conditioned to the academic tempo. Bumpus consistently exceeded that speed limit. He would get an idea about a circular to the alumni at breakfast, get it written and approved by lunch, and have presses printing it before his committee had finished their coffee. I soon learned that I was not doing my part if I was not prepared to mail eight thousand copies of it the following day. I never saw a man who could get into a problem farther and solve it more quickly with the tools immediately at hand than Bumpus. You will remember that in the campaign mentioned above he designed the Brown Bear Bonds, which were quite a success.

"At that particular period, I remember that Bumpus came up the hill reporting that a traffic officer had unjustly accused him of violating a traffic ordinance, and that he proposed to have him come up, hat in hand, and apologize for the language he had used. To my great surprise the policeman did exactly that on the following day. No one, not even a traffic policeman, could play fast and loose with Bumpus."

The Brown Bear Bonds were a typical product of Bumpus' fertile imagination. Bumpus well knew that when a donor makes a gift it is natural for him to desire some evidence of his generosity. Programs of symphony concerts and entertainments sponsored by philanthropic groups carry lists of patrons, and the blood donor receives a button or pin to attest his good deed. What could be more appropriate, then, than to give the alumnus or friend a bond, beautifully engraved, certifying his contribution to the cause and carrying the picture of a bear, the university mascot? The selling of these bonds made easier the work of the various committees and added a picturesque aspect to the drive. The campaign was a success, and the three-million-dollar fund was oversubscribed by some three quarters of a million.

Toward the end of the drive, when its ultimate success appeared doubtful, John D. Rockefeller, a Brown graduate of the class of 1897, sent a subscription of half a million dollars, which made it certain that the goal would be reached. Dr. Bumpus never forgot this handsome contribution. Later in life, when he did considerable work for the Rockefeller Foundation in connection with his service for the national parks, he consistently refused to accept any remuneration except his bare traveling expenses. In appreciation Mr. Rockefeller one Christmas wrote him the kindest of personal letters, with a check for a considerable amount enclosed.

True to his scientific training, Dr. Bumpus used the endowment drive for Brown as the medium for a little-publicized piece of research. Since all the alumni of the university were solicited, he undertook to learn what percentage of those who during their college career had received aid in the way of scholarships would respond to the appeal for contributions. If they contributed as little as a dollar to the fund their names were listed. It turned out that less than two per cent of such alumni felt any obligation for the assistance given them. As a result of this study Dr. Bumpus always held that it was wiser for the philanthropist interested in higher education to contribute directly to the college or university rather than to establish scholarships.

In Duxbury, as in every community where he resided for any length of time, Dr. Bumpus took an active part in civic affairs. The activities of the Duxbury Rural and Historical Society particularly appealed to him. He could always be counted upon to support actively any undertaking for the town's improvement, particularly when the preservation of its landmarks and historic heritage was concerned. In this endeavor he was ably assisted by Percy L. Walker, a real estate agent, who quietly and successfully contrived to see that undesirable persons and commercial projects were located elsewhere. Their combined efforts resulted in the town's retaining much of its delightful historic charm and attractiveness.

At the time of Duxbury's tercentenary celebration Dr. Bumpus headed a subcommittee for the publication of *The Story of Duxbury, Massachusetts*, sponsored by the Writers' Project of the Works Progress Administration. It gave him considerable satisfaction to pose during the celebration with his son and fifteen other citizens as one of the direct descendants of the original settlers.

For a number of years Dr. Bumpus had spent his summers in a house named "Curlew Cottage," located on the hill just above Plover, the cottage where his children and grandchildren summered. Climbing this hill several times daily became too strenuous for him in his later years, and so his older son purchased it in 1936, making it possible for him to acquire another residence. However, his interest in Curlew Cottage continued unabated, and he found as much pleasure in planning and improving the house and grounds for his children as he had for himself. When the contractors took over the house he merely transferred his interest to landscaping the grounds, and his daughter-in-law soon had one of the most beautiful gardens in Duxbury, a town noted for its gardens. Always interested in the unusual as well as the useful, he conceived the idea of laying out a garden at the water's edge. Building a low wall just at high-tide mark, he covered the plot with a foot or more of loam, and a beautiful and healthy flower garden soon replaced what had been an unsightly beach front.

Dr. Bumpus so enjoyed physical labor that during his last year of life he often lamented that he could not keep up his former pace. With his engaging smile he would protest, "My, what wouldn't I give for that delicious feeling of physical fatigue!"

After Curlew Cottage had been sold to his son, Dr. Bumpus purchased the historic house of Ezra Weston, better known as "King Caesar," who had been the most prominent and successful of the shipbuilders in the period from 1780 to 1840, when Duxbury had been a famous center of such maritime activity. King Caesar was also the owner of a fleet said at one time to number over ninety vessels—the largest fleet then under single ownership. At the height of his prosperity King Caesar built a pier and residence on Powder Point in Duxbury, where his ships could tie up in full view of his living room. Shortly after the close of the eighteenth century he sent to Paris for the finest of French wallpapers for the parlor, as a birthday present to his wife. After more than a hundred years it remains one of the outstanding examples of such decorative wallpaper in America and adds much to the charm and interest of the house. Much early American furniture of the finest type remained in the house. Augmented by the collection Dr. and Mrs. Bumpus had already accumulated, it made the house a veritable museum. Smaller buildings, including a ropewalk and a sail loft, surrounded the house, which had also a smugglers' cellar where old casks of Madeira had been stored after being carried around the world as ballast, for it was then believed that only long ocean voyages could impart to this wine the desired bouquet.

When Dr. Bumpus gained possession of this property, he was like a child with a new batch of toys. He went to work at once to turn the carriage shed into a summer cottage, and, departing this time from the names of birds, he called it "The Lodge." At one end of the living room he built a fireplace, and then suddenly, in the middle of construction, decided it was best to use this particular room as the kitchen. This change in plan made it necessary to place the refrigerator in the dining room and a lavatory at one end of the living room. The decorative furnishings were all Oriental materials he had himself collected. The ensemble, though unusual, had a certain attractiveness.

A young married couple who had seen The Lodge remarked to Dr. Bumpus' granddaughter, of whose relationship to him they were unaware: "You know, we were looking for a place to rent and saw one of the queerest houses you can imagine. An old man had put a fireplace in the kitchen and a washbasin in the living room, with the maid's room opening off the living room." Granddaughter Nancy retorted: "If you do as well as that when you are over eighty years old, you'll be doing pretty well. My grandfather built that house, and I like it!"

Building houses remained Dr. Bumpus' chief form of recreation. He told a friend that he had studied and taught so much that just to be able to use a hammer in a creative endeavor gave him the greatest pleasure. The last cottage he built was named "Coot," and here he spent his last summer, in bed most of the time because of his failing heart. But his bed was near the center of things, and he greatly enjoyed telling his visitors, as they came into the large front room, that the paneling around the fireplace had been in University Hall at Brown University, and that George Washington had undoubtedly sat before it when he visited there. In the bricks of this fireplace Dr. Bumpus had inserted four Delft tiles that he had picked up in a basement in Holland on his first European trip.

CHAPTER IX

Trailside Museums

UPON his retirement from the presidency of Tufts Dr. Bumpus looked forward to a life of comparative leisure, with opportunity to travel and at the same time keep in touch with those scientific bodies of whose governing boards he was a member. He disliked permitting his name to be associated with an undertaking unless he could pull his share of the load, and so he felt obligated to find the time to attend the numerous meetings demanded by such trusteeships. Obviously it was impossible for him to do so while he was president of a college, but after his retirement, besides the chairmanship of the Brown University endowment drive and his work for the museum of the American Red Cross, he kept in touch with the American Association of Museums, of whose Committee on Outdoor Education he was chairman. It was in this last position that he made the great contribution to the national parks embodied in the trailside museums.

An ardent advocate of conserving natural resources, he held that conservation was futile unless it was followed up by a program of public utilization and enjoyment. "Taken as a whole," he wrote, "and visited as they are by millions of people eager to learn, the National Parks of the United States offer the most attractive opportunity for adult education that now remains undeveloped. How shall the tourist be given the information that will render his visit educationally worth while? He is as keen for intellectual as he is for physical recreation. How shall the magnificent specimens in those roofless museums of nature be adequately labelled?"

Having conceived the idea of making virtually the whole country its own exhibit, he solved the problem of labeling by proposing that conveniently situated "interpreter houses," which he called "trailside museums," should serve as the labels. He believed that the surroundings of the museums, not the contents, were the exhibits, and that the museums should serve as sources of information about the works of nature that were left in their sites undisturbed. "Museum objectives have thus become inverted, but not upset," he remarked. In these trailside museums there were to be made available to the visitor exhibits that explained the surrounding region, with maps, pamphlets, guides, and a library of pertinent books.

Of these plans concerning outdoor education he wrote: "The controlling fact governing the development of educational work in the National Parks is that within these reservations multitudes are brought directly in contact with striking examples of nature's handicraft. To lead these people away from direct contact with nature, to beguile them into a building where they are surrounded by artifacts, and to subject them to the spell of the professional lecturer, is contrary to the spirit of this enterprise. The real museum is outside the walls of the building and the purpose of the museum work is to render the out-of-doors intelligible. It is out of this conception that a smaller specialized museum, the trailside museum, took its origin. While all parts of our National Parks are places of interest certain localities are especially inspiring, others have unusual teaching value, and still others outstanding scientific interest. The primary purpose of the trailside museum is to provide means that will enable the visitor on his arrival at a point of vantage to derive a moderate, if not a maximum amount of benefit. It is an 'insulation remover' and provides a hook-up between an object, or spectacle, charged with dynamic information and a mind receptive to informational impulses."

The first work of the American Association of Museums

with trailside museums was in Yosemite National Park, where at Glacier Point, more than three thousand feet above the valley floor, is located Glacier Point Lookout Station. Here are maps and charts that interpret the surrounding panorama, a telescope that brings distant objects into the near foreground, and collections that illustrate the physiography of the region. According to Dr. Carl P. Russell of the National Park Service, pioneer museums existed in Mesa Verde, Yosemite, and Yellowstone for several years before 1924, when the American Association of Museums extended its support to the Yosemite museum program.

Of Dr. Bumpus' way of working with the program Dr. Russell remarks: "Dr. Bumpus was always self-effacing in recording the progress of his personal undertakings. An example of his fairness in crediting the work of others is seen in his appraisal of his Committee's activities in the Yosemite Museum undertaking. In his report of 1926 he stated, 'The Yosemite project is one of several pieces of constructive work which the Association has done, but it has involved the cooperation of other organizations and of individuals both within and outside our membership. The Yosemite National History Association, the Yosemite Park & Curry Company have cooperated most zealously, the Sierra Club has lent its hand, the Superintendent of Yosemite and other ófficers throughout the National Park Service have helped most unselfishly and most efficiently. We have merely had a hand in bringing to completion a cooperative project. . . .' It was the great privilege of many naturalists, historians, and executives of the National Park Service to work closely with Dr. Bumpus throughout the period of his activity in national parks. His kindly guidance, mature judgment, fairness, brilliant learning, and constant friendliness meant much to those associated with him."*

The enthusiasm with which the Yosemite project was received by both the public and the National Park Service led

* *Yosemite Nature Notes*, December 1943, pp. 100–1.

the Committee on Outdoor Education to ask for funds for two more experimental trailside museums, one at Bear Mountain in the Palisades Interstate Park, some fifty miles north of New York City, and another at Yavapai Point in Arizona, on the rim of the Grand Canyon.

The development, equipment, and operation of the Bear Mountain station were largely determined by the officers of the American Museum of Natural History, who looked upon the station as a means of encouraging and directing urban youth in their efforts to get acquainted with the outdoor world. The attractive little building was set astride an excellently planned and efficiently maintained nature trail, of which it became, as Dr. Bumpus would have said, the "label."

At the Yavapai Point station the problems and objectives were quite different, for, in general, visitors to the Grand Canyon are adult rather than youthful, their minds are mature, and their stay is usually brief and not repeated. Moreover, here their attention is centered on a single magnificent and inspiring spectacle. Approximately 375,000 people approach this panorama every year and are moved by its majesty, and interpretation and understanding of this spectacle are only an enhancement of their emotion. The trailside museum at Yavapai Point was therefore planned, equipped, and operated as an observation station, with the purpose of calling attention briefly but accurately to the principal features of the canyon, to indicate the use of these features in reconstructing the history of the canyon and its future. A number of telescopes and view finders give the observer a glimpse of distant and salient positions; competent instructors and descriptive material interpret what may be seen; and models, charts, photographs, and carefully chosen specimens give other information of interest to the visitor.

So successful were these experimental trailside museums that the Laura Spelman Rockefeller Memorial made a grant to provide for a complete educational museum in Yellowstone

Park. This trailside museum, begun in the summer of 1928, was opened to the public in June 1929. Situated near Old Faithful, it was the first of a series of such buildings in strategic locations throughout the park.

Dr. Bumpus took as much interest in the actual planning and construction of the trailside museums as in their educational function. By choosing Herbert Maier as his architect and administrative associate he demonstrated again his instinct for getting exactly the right person to carry out the task in hand. The two became close friends through these joint endeavors, and some of Mr. Maier's most cherished possessions are letters from Dr. Bumpus signed "Dad."

The manner in which the attractive trailside museums blend into the natural landscape of the parks attests Mr. Maier's flair for this type of architectural work. The first museum at Yellowstone was built around a patio, with a covered rectangular passageway surrounding an area open to the sky. The walls of this passageway provide an excellent, well-lighted exhibition space where the story of Yellowstone's forests is told. The central area is devoted to a wild flower garden, and nearby is an outdoor auditorium in which evening lectures have a charm and intimacy conspicuously absent from the ordinary lecture room.

Sixteen miles down the Firehole River from Old Faithful is Madison Junction, where three rivers and three highways converge. Here in 1870 camped the Washburn party, after visiting Old Faithful, and here they resolved that this part of the country was unique and should be preserved inviolate as the common possession of the American people. This was the origin of the national park idea, since adopted by many nations. The museum at Madison Junction serves as a historic monument. On its southerly wall a large transparency depicts the Washburn party in camp, and other exhibits present historical data concerning the birth of the national park idea.

Dr. Bumpus instituted also the natural history shrines, in

which the construction and roadside location followed those of the religious shrines of Europe. But they contained, instead of religious images, information about nearby objects or natural phenomena. For example, beside a beaver dam near a highway there would be a shrine giving information about the dam-building and other habits of the beaver.

Dr. Bumpus' desire to point out to others the discoveries of science and the wonders of nature took on ever-increasing importance. Always eager to impart knowledge in a novel way, he wrote a series of guides for the Yellowstone motorist and hiker. These *Trailside Notes*, as he called them, were designed like a railroad folder, with markers along the margin, and described or called attention to things of note, mile by mile, between one museum and another. They were a self-service mileage guide that made the acquisition of knowledge a highly exciting game. These popular guidebooks have gone through innumerable printings. Concerning them and their author, Horace M. Albright, president of the American Planning and Civic Association and former director of the National Park Service, writes: "His easy association with young and old, rich and poor, the little schooled and the highly educated, gave him the background for his immensely successful museum technique, which, applied to national park museums and trailside exhibits, has so greatly increased tourist interest in the parks and monuments in recent years.

"I remember well the day he brought to me a copy of the *Trailside Notes* for the motorist and hiker from Mammoth to Old Faithful. This was issued in 1933, and was followed by notes for the Grand Canyon Desert View and West River Drives, and in 1942 by *Self-Guiding Auto Tour of Yosemite Valley*. I note that in none of these does the name of Dr. Bumpus appear. I suggest that in future editions which will be needed after the war, some note of recognition of the great service of Dr. Bumpus be incorporated."

J. E. Haynes, a close friend of Dr. Bumpus since the doctor's first visit to Yellowstone, wrote after his death:

"The work he did in Yellowstone will forever stand as a monument to his career. Time has shown that he acted wisely in the work he did."

Dr. Bumpus' reliance upon his own creativity, rather than upon tradition, habit, or counsel, explains his direct and original approach to the parks project, as to all the projects and problems he encountered. His own predilection throughout his life for things that could actually be seen made him confident that field exhibits are a more effective means of teaching than the conventional lecture. That this last undertaking, begun when he was past sixty years of age, should prove to be his greatest contribution to American education must be attributed mainly to his genius for ocular demonstration in the laboratory, in the museum, and under the open sky.

Since the desire for knowledge is not universal, Dr. Bumpus' endeavors to enlighten the general public were not always appreciated. In 1926, during a lecture in New York, he remarked that the trees on Boston Common might be a source of instruction to thousands seeking relaxation in that historic spot if the labels, which gave merely the scientific and common names, were expanded to include information on age, distribution, use, and origin. Realizing that Bostonians are sensitive about suggestions from outsiders, especially those from New York, the newspaper fraternity decided to rib the ardent educator. Cartoons appeared in the Boston papers depicting the type of citizen usually found on the Common, gazing at a label that read: "This is a tree. It is a tree because it isn't a cabbage. If it had pineapples on it, it would be a pineapple tree, but it hasn't and isn't. Last census gives it 118,711,331 leaves."

But such joshing in no way lessened Dr. Bumpus' enthusiasm for outdoor education in the national parks. He was fortunate to have become associated early in the work with Carl P. Russell, then Yosemite Park naturalist, later chief of the museum division, and afterward head of the branch of natural history of the National Park Service. With enthusiasm and the heartiest cooperation he helped Dr. Bumpus carry his ideas to a successful conclusion, and the museum division of the National Park Service grew from their combined labors.

In a chapter on trailside museums in *The Museum in America*, Laurence Vail Coleman writes of the work of the Committee on Outdoor Education of the American Association of Museums: "Hermon Carey Bumpus, as principal in this program, gave time and genius for a decade, becoming the father of museums in national parks. These beginnings have led to extensive results in the last few years. The federal government has already put in about two million dollars for buildings and exhibits. There are now about forty [more than one hundred in 1944] trailside museums in parks and other areas under control of the National Park Service. Scores are projected and it seems likely that each national reservation will have a museum or system of museums in time. The overrunning of this movement into state parks is now well under

Trees on Common Poorly Labeled

Boston cartoonists had a field day when Bumpus suggested fuller labels for the trees on the Common

way, and is especially important because there are so many areas of this kind. . . . The term 'trailside' coined by Bumpus suggests picturesquely that museums of this kind are field museums. Their essential character is that of being located where circumstances offer a subject to be explained, where nature provides an exhibit of earth formation or wild life, or man has left an archaeological or historic site."

Coleman adds in another chapter: "The philosophy of outdoor education is percolating into the thought of museum people everywhere. It is significant therefore, as Bumpus has said, that here is 'a new and large group of young and professionally trained men who are not primarily interested in quantitatively collecting, killing, preserving, transporting, storing, and exhibiting what have been called specimens, but who are primarily interested in qualitatively protecting, conserving and perpetuating natural conditions . . . to the end that those who so desire may enjoy the privilege of direct contact with original objective sources of information.' (*The Museum News*, June 15, 1937.)"*

And in the introductory pages of the *Field Manual* for museums in the National Park Service Ned J. Burns wrote: "Special thanks go to Dr. Bumpus, whose personal labors and discerning judgment have entered into the practical procedure and basic philosophy of park museum work from its early days to the present writing. This manual may well be regarded as evidence that the field museum program anticipated by Dr. Bumpus and his associates of the Committee on Outdoor Education is an established instrument in teaching Americans to know their heritage."

* *The Museum in America*. Washington: American Association of Museums. 1939.

CHAPTER X

National Park Service and Other Projects

THE trailside museum was only one of Dr. Bumpus' contributions to the development of the educational program of the national parks, which reached its maximum development in the years before World War II began. The first report of an informal educational committee appointed by Secretary of the Interior Ray Lyman Wilbur to consider the educational problems developing so rapidly in the parks proved so significant that he set up an advisory board to deal with the program. In 1931 Dr. Bumpus was elected chairman of this board, which met regularly during the next five years. During these years he worked as intensively in the field as around the conference table, and to his personal labors are traced many important features of the Park Service's interpretive method of education.

"He influenced us more than we realized at the time," Horace M. Albright writes, "for he never cared to claim credit for his accomplishments—his reward was to see his carefully formed policies adopted. Dr. Bumpus believed firmly that the National Park system was not yet complete. He saw that the increasing use of the parks and monuments meant that we should acquire, as we could, enough typical, qualified areas to serve our growing population without congestion."

This program showed further progress when in 1935 Congress passed the Historic Sites Act, authorizing the Secretary of the Interior to appoint an advisory body on national parks,

NATIONAL PARK SERVICE AND OTHER PROJECTS

historic sites, buildings, and monuments, and declared that in the future it would be the national policy to preserve for public use such places and objects of national significance. The advisory body so appointed was directed "to make a survey of historic and archaeologic sites, buildings, and objects for the purpose of determining which possess exceptional value as commemorating or illustrating the history of the United States," and "to develop an educational program and service for the purpose of making available to the public facts and information pertaining to American historic and archaeologic sites, buildings, and properties of national significance."

Dr. Bumpus was again made chairman of the committee, which was appointed by Secretary Harold L. Ickes, and during the next four years the committee held its meetings in various parts of the country in order to consider the relative merits of proposed sites for national parks and monuments. One of these meetings was held to investigate the desirability of establishing a park in the almost unknown wilderness of southern Florida. During the trip, by blimp and Navy patrol boats, a member of the party fell overboard as the boat rounded a sharp turn in a bayou, and the place was at once named "Bumpus Bend." This expedition led to the organization of the Everglades National Park project, in which Dr. Bumpus was keenly interested to the end of his life. Among many other such investigations, the committee considered the Big Bend region of Texas as a national park site, and in 1944, a year after Dr. Bumpus' death, it became the Big Bend National Park.

Dr. Bumpus' desire that the public should derive the maximum educational benefit from its institutions asserted itself even in the foreign field. Interviewed in London by a *Daily News* reporter, he mildly criticized some of the English museum methods and was reported as saying: "English museums contain the most wonderful material, but they always remain the same. In America a decided movement has been inaugurated to make the museums progressive. Museums should react to contemporary events. They should never be allowed to become stale. The curators of museums should illustrate with material at their command each event that bulks most largely in the common eye. Egyptology should, for instance, during the few weeks that public interest was roused to its highest by the Luxor discoveries, have displaced other subjects. That is the worst of English curators. Once some exhibition is placed under glass it remains there for ever. There it is, and there it stays. The whole secret of getting the most out of a museum is adapting it to the notice of the man in the street."

The British were no more grateful for such criticism than the Bostonians. A witty poem was their retort.

> Museums are wearisome places,
> The objects that there are on view
> Bring never a smile to the faces
> Of the solemn-eyed crowds that pass through.
> No wonder a Yankee professor
> Believes it would make a big hit
> If jolly old London, Lord bless 'er,
> Would jazz her museums a bit.
>
> The mummies of early Egyptians
> Are little relieved of their gloom
> By the recently posted inscriptions
> Of old King Tut-ankh-amen's tomb,
> But could one persuade the director
> To put on a crocodile dance
> With girls from the Pharaoh sector
> The place would be filled with romance.
>
> The same is quite true of the pictures
> By painters of glorious fame,
> Their figures though fine are but fixtures
> That never get out of the frame.
> Make cinema photographs of 'em—
> And we Yankees could do the job right—
> And the staidest of Britons would love 'em,
> They would buy out the house every night.

NATIONAL PARK SERVICE AND OTHER PROJECTS

> For scholars profound and pedantic
> An old style museum will do,
> But the lure of the gay and romantic
> Suits better the popular view.
> With African bands in the hallways,
> And dances on all the floors,
> The old institution will always
> Draw crowds to brave Albion's shores!

Even after he had reached the age of seventy Dr. Bumpus continued to make trips throughout the country in the interest of the Park Service. Arduous travel and long hours were the rule in such projects, but because of his great interest in such work and his sense of obligation to his country he accepted only out-of-pocket expenses for his efforts.

In October 1940, however, the increasing weakness of his heart made it necessary for him to resign from the service. To Secretary Ickes he wrote:

MY DEAR SECRETARY:

My physician has informed me that I must materially "reduce my tempo," and therefore I am asking you to allow me to resign from the membership on the Advisory Board to which you kindly appointed me some four years ago, and which followed a very pleasant connection with the National Park Service dating back to its adoption of an educational program initiated by the American Association of Museums in 1924.

It is with genuine regret that I thus abruptly break off my very agreeable official association with you and a delightful companionship and personal intimacy I have enjoyed with all members of the Board and with members of your staff in Washington and throughout the country. To have witnessed the wholesome, even marvellous, growth of a scheme of popular education—almost from its beginning has been a rare experience for which I am conscious of a deep sense of gratitude.

Always cordially and with best wishes,
H. C. BUMPUS

Upon learning of the letter all members of the board wrote Dr. Bumpus expressing their regret at his retirement, and at the next meeting the board passed a formal resolution expressing their esteem and affection.

HERMON CAREY BUMPUS

On April 24, 1941, the *New York Times* carried the following news item.

The annual awards of gold, silver, and bronze medals for distinguished Park Service were made yesterday by Alexander Hamilton, President of the Scenic and Historic Preservation Society, at a luncheon in the Federal Hall Museum, Sub-Treasury Building, Wall and Nassau streets.

The Cornelius Amory Pugsley Gold Medal for 1940 was awarded to Dr. Hermon C. Bumpus, past chairman of the Advisory Board of the National Park Service, for a long career devoted to education in the national parks.

In presenting the medal President Hamilton made the following remarks: "There is no group of public servants who deserve more generous recognition from the public than those whose lives are given over to the protection, development, and management of municipal, state, and national parks. . . . Never a highly paid pursuit, as payment for services rendered goes in this country, it is one of the professions which gives to its practitioners the greatest possible degree of personal satisfaction. For instance, my friend Dr. Bumpus, long an honorary member of our Society, must every day extract some measure of happiness from the knowledge that an idea of his—the trailside museum—is bringing enjoyment to a greater number of people every year.

"In other countries—Great Britain for example—there are various ways in which official, national recognition of outstanding service in the public interest may be rendered—by orders, titles, and the like—a most sensible and desirable arrangement, I have always thought. In our own democratic land, the function of hailing and approving outstanding achievement devolves upon societies like our own, but this makes the recognition none the less official or national in scope. . . .

"And now it is my most enjoyable duty to turn to, shall I say, one of the grand warriors . . . of the long fight for the public use of our national parks, Dr. Hermon Carey Bumpus.

NATIONAL PARK SERVICE AND OTHER PROJECTS

"I suppose the thing that makes me feel a warm bond between the doctor and myself is a discovery I made yesterday in refreshing my memory about the details of his career in the library of the *New York Times*. My discovery, and a most delightful one it was, was that he, too, once had some trouble over fish. That was back in 1911, when Dr. Bumpus was director of the American Museum of Natural History and a problem in ichthyology came up. The bone of contention was this: should fish be exhibited in a popular or a scientific manner? Dr. Bumpus was in favor of popularization; the powers that be preferred the scientific.

"I am glad to be able to report for those who may not recall the incident clearly that the doctor's attitude upon that occasion was progressively aggressive. He may even have been charged with a flavor of belligerence, and if he was I am sure he welcomed the impeachment. It seems to me that his whole career has been marked by that valuable quality— an intelligent belligerency in the public interest. He has sought steadily and successfully throughout his life to bring the treasures of the museum to the people and not the people to the museum. Today this point of view is a commonplace of modern museum techniques. In Dr. Bumpus we have one of the pioneers who first proposed the heresy and fought tooth and nail, sometimes at great personal sacrifice, for its adoption.

"His great contribution, of course, has been in the creation and popularization of the trailside museum. . . . He has never hesitated to take up the cudgels in the interests of the public, even when this involved a controversy with the British Museum and a criticism of the sacred trees on the Boston Common.

"I am sure you will understand, Dr. Bumpus, that in reciting some of the high lights of your past, I do so with the most profound admiration and, if the truth were known, a little envy. I love a scrapper, particularly one who does his fighting for the underdog, and until you came upon the scene the public was pretty much the underdog as far as museums were concerned.

"And because you have scrapped successfully in the public interest, I know that you are regarded with far more than admiration by the hundreds of thousands who visit our national parks each year and come away enlightened and instructed, and with a new appreciation and understanding of nature, as a result of your endeavors. By them you must be regarded with affection and with gratitude.

"I now take great pleasure in partially rewarding you by the presentation for outstanding service in the field of national park education of the Pugsley Gold Medal for 1940."

Dr. Bumpus had by no means lost interest in or severed his connection with the academic world during these years while he was engaged in the fascinating work of the National Park Service. In 1915 he had been elected to the American Academy of Arts and Sciences, and in 1939, against what must have been his better judgment in view of his failing health, he accepted a membership on the Tufts College Medical School Council. It was always difficult for him to refuse such an appointment when he felt he could be of assistance.

His great experience in educational matters was always available to and was frequently sought by the authorities of Brown University, who were making some fundamental changes in the organization and curriculum of the university. He was particularly fitted to be of assistance in such work, owing to his unique position as a graduate and past professor of Brown and for many years a member of its governing Board of Fellows. During his long life he held many positions of trust in the university he loved so well, and in his will was found a note to his elder son: "Brown has been awfully good to me—I request a substantial gift be made to its Biological Department."

One incident in the work he was quietly carrying on at

Brown was a source of considerable amusement to him. It had been decided to procure talent of international renown as head of a major department of the university, and accordingly Henry D. Sharp, a philanthropic citizen of Providence, later chancellor of the university, asked Dr. Bumpus to make a search in Europe. This inquiry among European universities proved fruitless, but on his return, much to his astonishment and gratification, he found the very man for the job not fifty miles from Providence.

Brown University made him secretary of the Corporation in 1924, and in 1927 members of the faculty, former students, and fellow alumni arranged for the painting of his full-length portrait, to be hung among other portraits of university worthies in Sayles Hall. The young artist, Howard E. Smith, at one time a teacher in Brown's School of Design, executed the portrait, and at the unveiling Dr. Bumpus' old friend and beloved associate of former years, A. D. Mead, then vice-president of the university, made the comment, "Like Leonardo, he has proved himself a master of interpretive physiognomy. Also he has established a record over all competitors, except Morpheus, by keeping Dr. Bumpus quiet for two consecutive hours without anaesthetics."

Early in the 1920's the New York State Legislature, largely as a result of the efforts of Chauncey J. Hamlin of Buffalo and other public-spirited citizens, appropriated a million dollars for the erection of a building for the Buffalo Society of Natural Sciences. Dr. Bumpus was invited to assume supervision of the planning of the new museum, and it was hoped that he could be persuaded to direct the institution. Though his interest in the wider field of the national parks would not permit the assumption of these full-time duties, he agreed to serve as consulting director and gave generously of his time in developing the plan of organization of the new museum. Though it was a distinct departure from general museum practices, his basic plan, calling for a series of individual exhibit halls each devoted to a separate and complete chapter in the story of science, was approved by the board of managers.

In 1930 John D. Rockefeller, Jr., requested him to make a survey of the Southwest, with a view to restoring and preserving the arts of the American Indian and setting up a program of education concerning them. Mr. Rockefeller is said to have remarked when he read Dr. Bumpus' report of the survey, "This is not what I asked for or expected, but it is most interesting." He was so impressed with Dr. Bumpus' suggestions that he established at Santa Fé the now well-known Laboratory of Anthropology, to be run along the lines of the Marine Biological Laboratory at Woods Hole. On April 22, 1931, he wrote in part to Dr. Bumpus: "You have surely started something in organizing the Laboratory. I believe it has a great future and am proud to be associated with it. What a satisfaction it must be to you to see already such worth-while results of your labors."

In commenting upon the great variety of Dr. Bumpus' activities, Thomas B. Appleget, vice-president of the Rockefeller Foundation, said: "That he moved about so much was not an indication of superficiality. In every job he took he made his complete and characteristic contribution. The sum total of his influence, because of this, is intangible but larger than if he had stayed in any one specialty. He was certainly never interested in routine administration. That I suppose is the reason why he was connected with so many different things—he made his contribution and moved on.

"There is no need of telling . . . what an affectionate and loyal friend he was, how wide his intellectual interests were, how bravely he defended his intellectual integrity, how much he enjoyed life, how undiscouraged he was by opposition and adversity. He could have achieved distinction in any one of the fields which he touched and he did achieve distinction in many of them."

CHAPTER XI

Indian Summer

AT A banquet at the Providence Art Club on May 5, 1932, in honor of Dr. Bumpus on his seventieth birthday, the librarian of Brown University, H. L. Koopman, read a poem he had written for the occasion.

> WHEN WILL BUMPUS BE OLD?
> How shall we know when Bumpus is old?
> Hark, and you shall hear the secret told.
> When he accepts the pace of the feet
> That shamble along the city street.
>
> But now, at three score years and ten,
> He pushes and dodges and pushes again
> As hard as ever he did before
> When his years were only a single score.
>
> Why does he rush? He has much to do,
> And loves to start it and push it through
> Just as he always did, and so,
> If we ever find him getting slow
>
> As the crowd he is fain to scold,
> Then we shall know that Bumpus is old.
> Yes, Time will slow down Bumpus yet,
> But not this decade—that is my bet!

He was right. Time did slow down Dr. Bumpus, but not until the next decade had almost passed.

To his friends Dr. Bumpus often expounded in considerable detail his belief that those who inhabit "this footstool of the Lord's," as he liked to call the earth, should not be handicapped in their endeavors by those who had gone before. He felt strongly that elder statesmen in any field should not make rules that would be binding on the following generation. It was his opinion that each new generation should solve its problems unencumbered by the ideas of either the aged or the dead.

Suiting his behavior to his belief, he followed his resignation from the National Park Service with his regretful withdrawal from the governing boards of many scientific societies with which his name had been associated.

Age did not make him lose, however, his alert concern for utilizing newer materials and more modern methods, and his interest in technical progress never failed. Of the hundreds of inventions and innovations that appeared during his lifetime the wrist watch was almost the only one to which he could not seem to accustom himself. His children recall that in the years when it was fashionable to wear watch chains draped tranquilly across the lower abdomen from one vest pocket to another—a chain on which, as on a back-yard clothesline, the less intellectual members of society hung Elk's teeth and Masonic emblems, while their more learned brethren substituted Phi Beta Kappa and Sigma Xi keys— Dr. Bumpus balanced his watch in one pocket with a small but powerful magnifying glass in the other. This glass was in constant use in the examination of animate and inanimate objects not easily observed by the naked eye.

As he grew older Dr. Bumpus indulged more and more the delight he had always taken in travel. He had purchased his first motorcar in 1906, when automobiles were hardly beyond the experimental stage, and had had the hardihood to take his family for a tour of the White Mountains the following summer. They often had to douse the brakes with bucketfuls of water before they could attempt to descend some of the hills, and changing the tires became a matter of almost daily routine.

Driving never seemed to tire the doctor, and he found so much of interest in the passing countryside that his compan-

Bumpus Butte, Yellowstone National Park

Bumpus in Yellowstone Park, where a trailside museum will be named for him

ions reveled in the free course in natural history he gave them. In the fall of 1936, at the age of seventy-four, he drove across the continent with Mrs. Bumpus to visit their sons in Southern California, stopping at many of the national parks along the way. On December 28 of that year they celebrated their golden wedding anniversary in Pasadena, where their granddaughter Nancy had that week been chosen queen of the Tournament of Roses. On their way back to the East they drove through the Southwest and visited the Laboratory of Anthropology in Santa Fé and the Big Bend country on the Texas border, and then continued as far south as Mexico City. Mexico had held a fascination for Dr. Bumpus ever since his trip to Yucatán in 1910, when he had journeyed to the prehistoric sites of the Mayas and Aztecs under the guidance of Dr. Thompson.

With the advent of air travel Dr. Bumpus first went aloft in 1926 on a trip from New York to Washington. This faster way of traveling had come none too soon for him, for he had accepted an invitation to work at the laboratory in Santa Fé, and his diary records no fewer than nine official visits during the same period to the Mt. Desert Biological Laboratory at Bar Harbor, Maine, as well as frequent trips to Buffalo.

Dr. Bumpus had purchased a winter home in St. Petersburg, Florida, and there he now pursued a hobby begun in his student days: organizing into permanent form genealogical data on the descendants of Edouard Bon Passe. Although he believed that "only imbeciles boast of their ancestors," his natural curiosity was a compelling factor in his search for knowledge about the kind of people he was descended from.

Of this pursuit he wrote: "Providence in Rhode Island is only about forty miles from Plymouth County, and the bicycle, in the early nineties, provided an attractive means of constructive recreation. There was joy in pedaling across country and in asking some rustic who looked like a Bumpus whether he really was one, and, if not, whether he could tell me where to find one. I had my notebook along and was unconsciously working myself into an alluring job. As a matter of fact, those informal and accidental contacts of fifty years ago, often with elderly people, provided me with information that it would now be impossible to obtain. I discovered that others were similarly employed and were quite willing to exchange their data for mine. Among these was Charles H. Bump of Longmeadow, Massachusetts, who had a natural talent for research and with whom or near whom our families spent two delightful winters in Florida. I found his work much superior to mine."

Whenever spring came Dr. Bumpus, like the birds, was anxious to get north to Duxbury, and late April or early May would invariably find him and Mrs. Bumpus in their summer home, the historic King Caesar house. Here he would take great pleasure in showing visitors the many fine examples of early American furnishings and in pointing out his handiwork in repairing and preserving the beautiful early nineteenth-century French wallpaper.

It was to the loft of the century-old barn, however, that he liked most to take his friends. In it he had fixed up a studio where he could enjoy working among the treasures he had collected during his long life. His mementos ranged from bits of Italian marble statues, brought to America as ballast in some early New England sailing ship, to Aztec relics recovered by divers from the depths of lakes in front of Aztec monuments. In prehistoric times human sacrifice was practiced at these spots, and the victims, with whatever ornaments they wore, were thrown into the lake.

In his quiet way he spent much of his time working for the welfare of Duxbury, and especially in keeping the charm of this south shore village from being spoiled by modern commerce. Among many more important things, he had his man of all trades plant and care for rambler roses along one of the public highways. Fond as he was of the town, what perhaps pleased him most was the fact that his grandchildren also loved this land of their fathers and anxiously counted the days until school would be over and they could come to Duxbury for their vacation.

Most of the family birthdays came in one week in August, and it was a family custom to celebrate them together. On such occasions Dr. Bumpus never failed to bring forth the unusual in gifts. Often it was some family heirloom. On the last occasion of this kind a small leather wedding trunk dated 1754, handed down through six generations, was the much prized gift to his granddaughter Nancy.

He was greatly pleased when his oldest grandson entered Brown University with the class of 1943, and immediately undertook to prepare one of the Duxbury lofts as a weekend cabin, with heat and hot water and bunks set up in a nautical manner. It was christened "Captain's Quarters," and was much appreciated by the college boys from Providence.

One of the family's chief recreations at Duxbury was sailing. Never a good sailor, however, Dr. Bumpus found life aboard his son's small schooner too confining for his restless nature. Though he took the greatest interest in the proposed itinerary of all cruises, he declined to go out except on afternoon sails, which he enjoyed mostly for the companionship they gave him with young people.

With the outbreak of World War II he followed the campaigns assiduously, and when one grandson joined the Naval Air Force and the other the Army Air Forces, their progress was a constant source of interest to him.

His physical condition grew progressively worse during the summer of 1942, which was again spent in Duxbury. Under rigid supervision, however, he recuperated sufficiently to return to his son's home in Pasadena in the fall. He spent that winter recording the family genealogy and correlating it with the chief historical and political events that had occurred during the lifetime of the various generations. At this time too he wrote the story of "Biology at Brown" at the request of his old associates—an account in which one must hunt carefully among the biographical notes for modest references to the chief actor in the play.

During this winter his first great-grandchild was born, and watching the baby develop was a constant source of joy to him. His room was on the ground floor and opened out on a garden filled with flowers, in which he also found much pleasure and interest. He often wrote letters to the United States Department of Agriculture, inquiring about certain plant diseases that had been puzzling the gardener, with whom he spent long hours discussing possible treatments.

In the spring of 1943 it became evident that his weakening heart would not permit his return to his beloved Duxbury. It was with profound regret that he wrote to the president of Brown University:

DEAR PRESIDENT WRISTON:

For something over sixty years I have been happy in feeling that I was a part of Brown. It has been a rich experience and it is with a wide range of regrets that I now ask you to present my resignation as Senior Fellow at the forthcoming meeting of the Corporation (June 2, 1943).

My reasons are as follows: There is doubt that I shall be able to attend future meetings of the Board. I feel that it is selfish for one to retain a nominal position of implied responsibility—may I say honor—and fail to discharge the incident obligations. At this most critical time in its history the University needs those who find satisfaction not alone in the achievements of the past but can look hopefully and confidently into the future, the period in which they are to live.

It is hard for me to give up the pleasant companionship with you and other members of the Corporation that I have so much appreciated and enjoyed, but I know that you will follow my wishes in my decision to retire from the Corporation at this time.

Always with best wishes,
HERMON C. BUMPUS

Pasadena, California
May 22, 1943

Upon receipt of this letter the Corporation abandoned the

precedent of 175 years to do honor to Dr. Bumpus: They elected him the first Fellow Emeritus of the university, in order that he might have all the privileges and courtesies, without any of the duties, of membership on the Board of Fellows. President Wriston's letter informing him of this action, which arrived only a day before he was taken to the hospital in his last illness, gave him deep pleasure.

In the first week of June 1943 he experienced a severe heart attack and was taken to a hospital to receive the best possible care. During his short illness his unusual personality, cheerful smile, and universal interest made a profound impression on the hospital personnel. He died on June 21, 1943.

His life is well summarized in these sentences written by his oldest and most intimate friend, Dr. A. D. Mead: "Dr. Bumpus thoroughly enjoyed his stay upon this planet, which he found so full of a number of things. He enjoyed pointing out these things in a new light to the men, women, and children, high and low, who were here in his time, and he did not neglect the interests of those yet to arrive.

"At the last, he went on his way in a golden sunset, aware that what he had done and the motive of it had won approval in the judgment of his peers."

Appendix

MEMORIALS AND RESOLUTIONS

Resolution Passed by the Advisory Board, National Park Service

THE Advisory Board of the National Park Service, meeting in Washington, learns with profound regret that Dr. Hermon C. Bumpus, Chairman of the Board since its creation, has found it necessary, for reasons of health, to withdraw from his office and membership on the Board.

The Advisory Board is humbly conscious of the distinguished service that, with complete and self-sacrificing devotion, Dr. Bumpus has rendered to the Board and to the National Park Service over many years. As a member and Chairman of the special Advisory Board that was the predecessor of the present Board, Dr. Bumpus was a pioneer in the task of developing the educational program of the National Park Service. During his long service he spent freely of his time and effort, and of the results of his lifetime experience in making available to the people of the United States the educational, recreational, and spiritual resources of their country's scenic and historical areas and monuments. His special knowledge and his wisdom have been invaluable in setting and maintaining the highest standards for the scientific and educational work of the National Park Service; his personality has made him beloved not only by his fellow members of the Board, but by the entire staff of the Service.

The Board expresses its great esteem and affection for its retiring Chairman, its best wishes for his own work and his personal wellbeing, and its hope that it may continue to profit by his lively interest in its activities.

October 28, 1940

Memorial to Hermon Carey Bumpus Adopted by the Corporation of Brown University at Their Meeting of October 25, 1943

The Corporation of Brown University records its keen sense of loss in the death of Hermon Carey Bumpus, Fellow Emeritus. It records its sincere gratitude for his great devotion to the welfare of the University through very many years, and its pride in his stewardship of the rich talents which Nature, his home, and his Alma Mater gave into his keeping. It records its genuine esteem and affection engendered by intimate acquaintance with his sterling and lovable human traits.

He died on June 21, 1943, at Pasadena, the home of his elder son, at the ripe age of 81 years. He was in full vigor of mind and spirit until his failing heart could no longer carry its burden.

For more than three score years the welfare of Brown had been among his foremost concernments, and during more than fifty of these years he was officially a member of the academic family as student, Professor, Fellow, Secretary of the Corporation, and finally as Fellow Emeritus.

He was graduated from Brown in 1884. After two years as assistant to Professors Packard and Jenks, and five years as professor at Olivet College, he went to Clark University, then newly founded, to pursue his graduate studies. He received from Clark the Ph.D. degree, being the first recipient of a degree from that institution. Of greater significance to Brown, he received, from his association with that noble assembly of scholars at Clark, a baptism in the traditions and ideals of European scientific scholarship at its very height.

As one of President Andrews's first appointees, he returned to Brown in 1890, and with steady vision directed his dynamic energy to proving that, in his field of work at least, the ideals of teaching and the ideals of research could be united with mutual benefit. The demonstration and the influence of his continuous espousal of this doctrine were of eventual consequence to Brown.

He resigned from his professorship in 1900, became the first Director of the American Museum of Natural History in New York, and eventually the foremost figure in museum education in America.

Once more he was brought into official connection with Brown by his election to the Board of Fellows in 1905. In 1924 he accepted appointment also as Secretary of the Corporation, a position he held until 1937. As a member of the Board of Fellows to whom the charter assigns the responsibility for educational policy, and by reason of his wide experience and his intimate acquaintance with the particular conditions at Brown University, he exerted a great influence upon the progressive development of the University for more than a generation.

The same vision, executive ability, and inspiring personality that characterized his career at Brown marked also his achievements in the several major educational enterprises which he was afterwards called to direct. Into all of them he brought fresh, original, invigorating ideas and played a leading part in establishing or remodeling educational policies and procedures. In all of them there still abide among his former associates appreciative memories of his personal inspiration, so well expressed in the recent happy phrase of his old colleagues in the American Museum of Natural History: "Remembrance of Dr. Bumpus is here still green and flourishing, despite the long generation that has passed since he labored among us. Wherever he directed the light of his mind, he left perpetual illumination, a fact that applies alike to institutions and to the hearts of his fellow workers."

His Alma Mater, while mourning the loss of a loyal and devoted son, rejoices in the fullness of years which was vouchsafed him and in the enlightenment which he brought to millions of his fellow men, in the high place which he attained both in the judgment of his peers and in the affection of friends without number.

Memorial Adopted by the American Association of Museums at Their Annual Meeting, February 11, 1944

The Council of the American Association of Museums records its sorrow and deep sense of loss in the death of Dr. Hermon Carey Bumpus, fellow councilor and friend, first president of our Association, ever a wise and strong advocate of the best in museums as in all things.

He died June 21, 1943, in Pasadena, California, at the age of eighty-one years. He spent forty-two years in the service of museums as worker, trustee, and officer.

Through the American Museum of Natural History, of which he was the director for nearly a decade, he contributed to cultural life and by his influence he advanced the standing of museums everywhere.

Through the National Parks, to which he devoted himself for the closing decade and a half of his life, he carried forward an inspired plan of outdoor education based on nature's works and on scenes of history.

During the years between these times he piled achievement upon achievement. Universities, professional societies, scientific establishments including the Marine Biological Laboratory at Woods Hole, as well as museums, were the beneficiaries of his genius and abounding energy.

APPENDIX

He lived the good life, and the world is lastingly better for his having lived. We who have been his colleagues hail his distinguished services and give tribute reverently to his memory.

Resolution Adopted by Tufts College Teachers' Association, October 26, 1940

On the occasion of its twenty-fifth Annual Meeting the Tufts College Teachers' Association records its sincere appreciation and commendation of the distinguished career of

HERMON CAREY BUMPUS

Ph.B., Brown University, 1884
Ph.D., Clark University, 1891
Sc.D., Tufts College, 1905
Sc.D., Brown University, 1905
LL.D., Clark University, 1909

President of Tufts College, 1914–1919; Master Teacher and Administrator in the field of University Education; Founder of this Association, which herein and hereby cites with affectionate pride his many accomplishments.

Testimonial Presented by Tufts College Graduates January 9, 1919

In grateful appreciation for the loyal and unselfish thought and labor which Hermon Carey Bumpus has given Tufts College and her varied interests, the graduates of Tufts in every walk of life throughout the country speak their admiration and affectionate regard. Under his leadership as president Tufts College has become a greater and more potent factor in service to mankind and to the country. This expression of esteem and gratitude is presented to the end that the sentiment of Tufts graduates may be forever engraved upon his memory.

A Tribute from the Staff of the American Museum of Natural History

[The following telegram was sent at the time of Dr. Bumpus' death to his two sons, Doctors H. C. Bumpus, Jr. and L. D. Bumpus, in Pasadena, California.]

Old friends and associates of your father on the staff of the American Museum of Natural History, both active and retired, join in tribute to his career and character and in an expression of deepest sympathy to your mother and all other members of the family. Remembrance of Dr. Bumpus is here still green and flourishing, despite the long generation that has passed since he labored among us. Wherever he directed the light of his mind, he left perpetual illumination, a fact that applies alike to institutions and to the hearts of his fellow workers.

Roy Chapman Andrews
Albert E. Butler
Frank M. Chapman
James L. Clark
W. M. Faunce
William K. Gregory
Frank E. Lutz

Roy W. Miner
Robert Cushman Murphy
John Treadwell Nichols
Henry C. Raven
Fred H. Smyth
A. H. Summerson
Clark Wissler

MEMBERSHIPS AND OFFICES

American Association for the Advancement of Science, from February 1901; elected member January 18, 1905; fellow, 1906–43; local executive committee, 1907 meeting.

American Association of Museums, active member from April 1906; president, 1906.

American Bison Society, member board of managers from February 1907.

American Fisheries Society, member from 1897.

American Forestry Association, active member from November 2, 1906; resigned January 7, 1909.

American Free Art League.

American Geographical Society, elected fellow November 23, 1909.

American Institute of the City of New York.

American Morphological Society, member 1890–1902; vice-president, 1900; president, 1902.

American Museum of Natural History, assistant to president, curator of invertebrates, 1901–2; director, 1902–11; elected patron November 14, 1904.

American Nature Study Society, member from March 1908.

American Philosophical Society, elected February 1901, but owing to failure to acknowledge receipt of notification name was withdrawn and membership lapsed; elected again April 1909; elected member Committee on South Polar Exploration October 15, 1909.

American Red Cross, museum committee.

APPENDIX

American Scenic and Historic Preservation Society, elected corresponding member June 22, 1908; secretary.
American School of Prehistoric Research, trustee, 1928-31.
American Society of Naturalists, elected member December 30, 1886; secretary, 1895-98; vice-president, 1899.
American Society of Zoologists (successor to American Morphological Society), member from 1903; president, 1903.
Audubon Society of Rhode Island, president, 1897-1901; resigned March 1902; honorary president, 1941-43.
Audubon Society of the State of New York, member of executive committee before incorporation in 1904; member board of directors from December 1904; vice-president, 1905, 1906, 1908, 1909.
Boone and Cròckett Club, associate member from January 1910.
Boston Society of Natural History, corporate member.
Brooklyn Institute of Arts and Sciences, board of managers (Cold Spring Harbor) from May 1902; resigned January 1909; resignation withdrawn January 22, 1910.
Brown University, Ph.B., 1884; instructor and graduate student, 1884-86; assistant professor of zoology, 1890-91; associate professor, 1891-92; professor of comparative anatomy, 1892-1900, and member of various committees; honorary D.Sc., 1905; board of fellows, 1905; secretary of Corporation, 1924-36; fellow emeritus, 1943.
Brown University Club in New York, member 1901-10; board of governors, 1904; president, March 1907-February 1908.
Buffalo Museum of Sciences, consulting director, 1924-30.
Butler Hospital, member of Corporation.
Century Club (Association), resident member from February 1, 1902; committee on admissions.
Children's Museum of Brookline, Massachusetts, trustee.
City Club of Boston, board of governors, 1924.
Columbia University, appointed member of Faculty of Pure Science April 1905 (ex officio member as director of American Museum of Natural History).
Committee on Congestion of Population in New York, executive and general committee; resigned October 1908.
Committee on Libraries and Museums, Child Welfare Exhibit, April 1908.
Delta Phi, Beta Chapter, member of Corporation from 1908; board of governors.
Duxbury Local Defense, chairman of committee.
Duxbury School Board.
Ends of the Earth, elected active member December 1909.

Examiners Club, Boston.
Fortnightly Club, elected December 1906.
Historic Sites, appointed to advisory board by Secretary of the Interior Ickes December 1935.
Home for the Feeble-minded, Waverly, trustee.
International Congress of Americanists, held in New York in 1902; in Mexico, 1910.
International Congress of Arts and Sciences, invitation to membership, St. Louis Exposition, September 1904.
International Congress of Zoology (Seventh), Boston.
International Fisheries Congress (Fourth), held in Washington, 1908; delegate for the state of New York; president.
International Peace Congress, member local advisory committee from February 1907.
Jefferson Expansion Memorial, 1939.
K. K. Oesterreichische Fischerei-Gesellschaft (Vienna), elected honorary member December 1908.
Laboratory of Anthropology, Santa Fé, organizer, 1926; honorary trustee, 1939–43.
Linnaean Society of New York, resident member from December 1918.
Marine Biological Laboratory, Woods Hole, instructor, 1892; assistant director, 1894–95; secretary of Corporation, 1897–99; board of trustees, 1897–1942.
Massachusetts Security League, chairman.
Men's Club, First Presbyterian Church, New Rochelle, New York, resigned October 1908; North Avenue Presbyterian Church, New Rochelle.
Metropolitan Museum of Art, honorary fellow from February 1909.
Middlebury College (Vermont), honorary alumnus from August 1906.
Mount Desert Laboratory, Bar Harbor, Maine, trustee, 1924–43.
National Association of Audubon Societies, incorporator, 1905; director, 1904–7, also 1907–12; member executive committee, board of directors, February 1905; sustaining member from October 1908.
National Geographic Society, member from November 1904.
National Park Service, chairman Educational Advisory Board, 1931–40; chairman of Museums; chairman Outdoor Education, 1925.
National Society for the Promotion of Industrial Education, 1906.
New England Society in the City of New York, elected to member-

APPENDIX

ship January 15, 1908; resigned November 17, 1909; resignation withdrawn 1910.

New Rochelle Board of Education, 1908–11; Committee Playground Congress, 1910.

New York Academy of Sciences, elected resident member February 1901; elected fellow February 1902; recording secretary, 1905, 1909; councilor, 1906, 1907, 1908; corresponding secretary, Committee on Honorary and Corresponding Members and Fellows, January 1909; headquarters committee, January 1910; delegate to Eighth International Zoological Congress at Graz, Austria, 1910.

New York Botanical Garden, elected annual member May 1902.

New York Society of the Archaeological Institute of America, member from February 1910.

New York Zoological Society, elected annual member October 1901; elected fellow May 1909.

Pathological Institute of the New York State Hospitals, advisory board, 1901.

Peace Society of the City of New York, annual member from April 1907; resigned January 1909.

Peary Arctic Club, elected member December 1907.

Phi Beta Kappa, elected member of Alpha Chapter of Rhode Island (Brown University), 1891.

Playground Association of America, vice-president National Congress, New York, September 1908; vice-president Third American Congress, Pittsburgh, May 1909.

Providence Art Club, member; honorary member, 1940.

Public Health Defense League, November 1907.

Rhode Island Commissioners of Inland Fisheries, member 1897–1901.

Rhode Island Hospital, board of trustees, 1895–1901; resigned 1901.

Rhode Island Medical Society, honorary member from 1898.

Rhode Island School of Design, member board of management 1899–1901, resigned 1901; associate member, 1901; member of Corporation from 1902, resigned January 1908.

School of American Archaeology (Archaeological Institute of America), elected to managing committee December 19, 1909.

School Garden Association of New York, member committee of organization from January 1908; vice-president, 1908, 1910.

Senkenbergische Naturforschende Gesellschaft, Frankfurt, Germany, corresponding member from October 13, 1907.

HERMON CAREY BUMPUS

Sigma Xi, Brown University Chapter, charter member from May 1900; president, 1933.
Society for the Advancement of India, board of trustees, March 1908; resigned.
Somerville Public Library, trustee.
State Advisory Council of Adult Education, Commonwealth of Massachusetts.
Tufts Dental Alumni Association, honorary member, 1915.
University Club, Providence, member; board of governors; resigned from club Septen ; 1908.
Washington Academy of Sciences, nonresident member 1901-9.
Wilderness Society, president.

PAPERS AND ADDRESSES

A simple and inexpensive self-registering auxanometer. *Botanical Gazette*, vol. 12, no. 7, 1887.
The embryology of the American lobster. *Journal of Morphology*, vol. 5, 1891.
A Laboratory Course in Invertebrate Zoology. New York: Henry Holt, 1893.
The median eye of adult crustacea. *Zoologisch Anzeiger*, no. 447, 1894.
Instinct and education in birds. *Science*, n.s., vol. 4, no. 86, 213-17, August 21, 1896.
A contribution to the study of variation: skeletal variations of *Necturus Maculatus* Raf. *Journal of Morphology*, vol. 12, no. 2, 1897.
The variations and mutations of the introduced sparrow, Passer domesticus; a second contribution to the study of variation. Biological lectures at the Marine Biological Laboratory at Woods Holl, 1897.
The Importance of Extended Scientific Investigation. Washington: Bulletin of the U.S. Fish Commission for 1897.
On the reappearance of the tile-fish, Lopholatilus chamaeleonticeps. *Science*, n.s., vol. 8, no. 200, 1898.
Professor James Ingraham Peck. *Science*, n.s., vol. 8, no. 783, 1898.
The variations and mutations of the introduced Litorina; a third contribution to the study of variation. *Zoological Bulletin*, vol. 5, 1898.
Work at the biological laboratory of the U.S. Fish Commission at Woods Holl. *Science*, n.s., vol. 8, no. 186, 1898.

APPENDIX

On the identification of fish artificially hatched. *American Naturalist*, vol. 32, no. 378, 1898.

The elimination of the unfit as illustrated by the introduced sparrow, Passer domesticus; a fourth contribution to the study of variation. Biological lectures at the Marine Biological Laboratory, 1898.

The breeding of animals at Woods Holl during the months of March–September, 1898. *Science*, n.s., vols. 7–9, nos. 171, 177, 185, 207, 225, 1898–99.

Notes on the times of breeding of some common New England nemerteans. *Science*, n.s., vol. 9, no. 214, 1899.

Facts and theories of telegony. *American Naturalist*, vol. 33, no. 396, 1899.

Methods and results of scientific work at Woods Holl. Presented at twenty-eighth annual meeting of the American Fisheries Society, 1899.

The Reappearance of the Tile-fish, Lopholatilus. Washington: Bulletin of the U.S. Fish Commission for 1898. [1899.]

On the movements of certain lobsters liberated at Woods Holl. Contributions from the biological laboratory of the U.S. Fish Commission, 1900.

The results attending the experiments in lobster culture made by the U.S. Commission of Fish and Fisheries. *Science*, n.s., vol. 14, no. 365, 1901.

The museum as a factor in education. *Independent*, 61:269–72, August 2, 1906.

The great American museum. *World's Work*, 15:10027–36, March 1908.

Darwin and zoology. *Popular Science*, 74:361–66, April 1909.

Efficiency in the university. *School and Society*, 1:664–67, May 8, 1915. Same, *Education*, 35:660–64, June 1915.

Installation of the president of Tufts College. *School and Society*, 1:881–82, June 19, 1915.

Obligations of the trustees, faculty and alumni to the college. *School and Society*, 2:73–81, July 17, 1915.

Problem of adjustment of higher education to the needs of the state. *Education*, 36:288–95, January 1916.

Vinal N. Edwards. *Science*, n.s., 50:34–35, July 11, 1919.

Relations of museums to the out-of-doors. *Playground*, 21:329–33, September 1927.

Trailside museums. *Parents' Magazine*, 4:32, June 1929.

Hobbies. *Magazine of the Buffalo Museum of Sciences*, vol. 10, no. 10, 1930.

Museum work in the national parks. *Museum News*, vol. 7, no. 14, 1930.
Trailside museums. *Museum Journal*, vol. 30, 1930.
Everglades Park. *Review of Reviews*, 85:48, March 1932.
Trailside Notes. Washington: National Park Service, U.S. Department of the Interior. No. 1, 1933; no. 2, 1936.
Objectives of museum work in national and state parks. *Museum News*, vol. 15, no. 4, 1937.

ARTICLES ABOUT HERMON CAREY BUMPUS

Portrait. *World's Work*, 12:7694, July 1906; 16:10401, July 1908.
Neglected paper on natural selection in the English sparrow; Professor Bumpus on elimination of the unfit. J. A. Harris in *American Naturalist*, 45:314–18, May 1911.
Obituary. *School and Society*, 57:703, June 26, 1943. *Science*, 99:28–30, January 14, 1944. By A. M. Mead.

Index

Agassiz, Louis, 18, 26
Akeley, Carl, 57–58, 104–5
Albright, Horace M., 108, 112
American Association of Museums, 68, 71–72, 103, 110–11, 115
American Museum of Natural History, 12, 53, 54–72, 79, 93, 106
American Red Cross, 97, 103
Andrews, E. Benjamin, 35, 39–40, 43, 83
Andrews, Roy Chapman, 63–64
Annisquam, biological laboratory, 21, 26
Appleget, Thomas B., 97–98, 120
Arnold, Oliver H., 44

Baird, Spencer F., 27, 28, 29
Bates, Chester, 95–96
Biological Club, Providence, Rhode Island, 44
Bon Passe, Edouard, 3, 96, 123
Bonsall, Captain, 63
Boston Common cartoons, 109, 110
Brown University, 14–15, 17–21, 22, 35–53, 61, 66–67, 74, 76, 83, 88, 95, 97–99, 102, 118, 119, 125, 126–27; biology department, 35–44, 50–52, 118, 125–26
Buffalo Society of Natural Sciences, museum, 119–20, 123
Bumpus, Abbie Eaton, 5, 7, 9, 12–13, 16
Bumpus, Hermon Carey: American Academy of Arts and Sciences, elected, 118; American Association of Museums, president, 68, Committee on Outdoor Education, chairman, 103; American Morphological Society, vice-president, 53; American Museum of Natural History, assistant to president and curator, 53, 54–59, director, 59–72, resignation, 71; American Red Cross, museum for, 97, 103; American Society of Naturalists, vice-president, 53; ancestry, 3–10; Audubon Society of Rhode Island, president, 45; "Biology at Brown," author, 41–43, 125–26; birth, 3–4; Boston Common cartoons, 109, 110; Boston Society of Natural History, member, 52; boyhood, 5–16; British retort to criticism, 114–15; Brown University—board of fellows, member, 95, 127, Brown Bear Bonds, designer, 98, Corporation, member, 119, resigned from, 126, endowment drive, 97–99, fellow emeritus, 126–27, portrait in Sayles Hall, 119, professor, 35–53, student, 17–21; Buffalo Society of Natural Sciences, museum, consulting director, 119–20, 123; builder and designer of houses, 92–102; Columbia University, faculty, 69–70; Commander's Cross, Roumania, transmitted, 68; death, 127; Duxbury, Massachusetts, summer home, 88, 94–97, 99–100, 101, 124–25; education, 10, 12, 14–15, 17–21, 24; European travel, 43, 67–68; Gaekwar of Baroda, friendship, 73–78; gardening, 92, 100, 126; genealogy, interest in, 1, 123–24, 125; grandchildren, 20, 96, 100, 101–2, 123, 125; great-grandchild, 126; honorary degrees, 66–67; horticulture, interest in, 12, 92; ideas, originality in presenting, 11–12, 58, 61, 63; International Fisheries Congress, president, 34; Kent Diploma, conferred, 71–72; Laboratory of Anthropology, Santa Fé, organizer, 120, 123; later years, 121–27; life, summarized by Mead, 127; marriage, 23; *Men of Science*, listing, 70; Mexico and Yucatán, trip to, 63, 123; Mt. Desert Biological Laboratory, official visits to, 123; National Association of Audubon Societies, director, 53; National Committee for Bird Protection, chairman, 52–53; National Parks, work with, 103–11, 112–18; natural history shrines, originator, 107–8; nature, early interest in, 6, 7, 10, 13–14; outdoor education, 103–11; Pasadena, California, last

days at, 125–27; Phi Beta Kappa, member, 52; practical education, interest in, 10–11; Pugsley Gold Medal, awarded, 116–18; Quartermaster Corps, work in, 89; research and scientific investigations—biometrical studies, 46–49, English sparrow, 46–47, 47–48, flatfish fry, 30, garter snake, embryonic development of, 22, *Litorina littorea*, variability in, 47, lobsters, 24, 30–32, *Necturus*, skeletal structure of, 27, 49, scholarship aid and alumni contributions, 99, tilefish, rediscovery of, 32–34, X-ray studies, 49; Rhode Island Commission on Inland Fisheries, member, 51–52; Rhode Island Hospital, board of trustees, member, 44, X-ray work at, 49; Rhode Island Medical Society, honorary member, 44; Rhode Island School of Design, board of management, member, 44–45; Rockefeller Foundation, work for, 99; scientific papers by, 28–34, 45–50; seventieth birthday, banquet honoring, 121; Sigma Xi, member, 52; summer homes, 92–94, 100–2, 124; teacher, at Brown University, 35–53, at Olivet College, 21–23; trailside museums, originator, 103–11; *Trailside Notes*, 108; travel, 43, 63, 67–68, 103, 122–23; Tufts College, president, 82–91, Medical School Council, member, 118; U.S. Bureau of Fisheries, scientific director, 27–34; University of Wisconsin, business manager, 71, 79–82; Waban, Massachusetts, house in, 94; winter home, St. Petersburg, Florida, 123; Woods Hole Marine Biological Laboratory—assistant director, 25–27, board of trustees, member, 26, scientific studies produced at, 45–47

Bumpus, Hermon Carey, Jr., 23, 39, 43, 75–78, 89, 93, 94, 118, 125
Bumpus, Laurin Aurelius, 4–10, 15–16
Bumpus, Lucy Ella Nightingale, 23, 40, 43, 76, 94, 123, 124
Burns, Ned J., 111

Carmichael, Leonard, 88–89
Carnegie, Andrew, 63
Chapman, Frank M., 53, 62–63

Clark, James L., 57–58
Clark University, 23–24, 25, 35, 53, 67
Clarke, Sir Caspar Purdon, 63
Coleman, Laurence Vail, 110–11
Collar, Alice, 14
Cullis Mission and Repository, 6–9, 12
Curie, Marie and Pierre, 66

Darwin, Charles, 19, 45–48
De Forest, Robert, 63
Dohrn, Anton, 25, 43
Duxbury, Massachusetts, 3, 88, 94–97, 99–100, 101, 124–25

Eliot, Charles W., 63
Endicott, William E., 10

Faunce, W. H. P., 66, 97
Field Museum, Chicago, 57–58
Fish Hawk, 28
Franklin, Sir John, 63

Gaekwar of Baroda, 73–78
Gompers, Samuel, 63
Gould, Helen, 63
Grampus, 28, 33–34
Gray, George M., 26–27
Grey, Earl, 63

Hale, Edward Everett, 63
Hale, George E., 15
Hall, G. Stanley, 24
Hamilton, Alexander, 116–18
Hamlin, Chauncey J., 119
Harris, J. A., 48 (note)
Harvard University, 76–78, 83
Hassam, Childe, 10
Haynes, J. E., 108–9
Heilprin, Angelo, 63
Hensen, Matt, 65–66
Hoffman, Ralph, 53
Huxley, Julian, 48 (note)
Hyatt, Alpheus, 21

Ickes, Harold L., 113, 115

Jasingrao, Prince, 75–78, 94
Jenks, J. W. P., 14–15, 18, 20
Jesup, Morris K., 53, 55–56, 59, 64, 71, 73

Kane, Elisha Kent, 63

INDEX

Kellogg, James L., 22-23
Knight, Charles H., 57
Koopman, H. L., 121

MacKenzie, De Witt, 73
Madison, Wisconsin, 81, 83, 95
Maier, Herbert, 107
Massachusetts Institute of Technology, 41
Mead, A. D., 29, 31, 32, 34, 36, 52, 88, 119, 127
Metropolitan Museum of Art, 54, 55
Mills, D. O., 63
Morgan, J. P., 54-55
Mt. Desert Biological Laboratory, 123
Murphy, Robert Cushman, 61-62

Narragansett Bay, biological survey of, 42-43, 51
National Fisheries Congress, 28
National Parks, 103-11, 112-18

Olivet College, 21-23, 24

Packard, Alpheus Spring, 19, 20, 50
Page, Walter, 63
Peary, Robert E., 64
Peary Arctic Club, 64
Penikese marine laboratory, 25-26
Pierce, John, 41
Pinchot, Gifford, 63
Pritchett, Henry S., 81-82

Radeke, Gustave, 44
Robinson, Ezekiel Gillman, 17-19, 35
Rockefeller, John D., 63
Rockefeller, John D., Jr., 99, 120
Rockefeller Foundation, 97, 99, 120

Rockefeller Memorial, Laura Spelman, 106
Roosevelt, Theodore, 34
Russell, Carl P., 105, 109-10

Sharp, Henry D., 119
Sherwood, George H., 61
Smith, Howard E., 119
Southwick, James W., 37
Spicer, William, 76
Stefansson, Vilhjalmur, 66

Tilefish, 32-34
Tower, Ralph W., 66
Trailside museums, 103-11
Trautman, James F., 82-83
Tufts College, 67, 82-91, 95, 103, 118

U.S. Bureau of Fisheries laboratory, 27-33
University of Wisconsin, 71, 79-82

Van Hise, President, 79, 80
Veeder, Captain Bob, 33, 34

Walter, Herbert Eugene, 37-39
Weston, Ezra ("King Caesar"), 100-1
Wheeler, William Morton, 83-84
Whitman, Charles Otis, 25
Whitnach, Ralph C., 74
Wilbur, Ray Lyman, 112
Wilder, Marshall P., 12
Wilson, J. Walter, 48 (note)
Wissler, Clark, 71-72
Woods Hole Marine Biological Laboratory, 25-27, 35-36, 50, 54, 61, 120
Wriston, Henry M., 126-27

www.ingramcontent.com/pod-product-compliance
Lightning Source LLC
Chambersburg PA
CBHW061451300426
44114CB00014B/1935